78358   E
                     169.12
Wylie   W9

Sons and daughters of mom

Date Due

FE 15'73			
AP 16'73			
AP 24'74			
MAY 20 '75			
AUG 19 '75			
FEB 10 '78			
JAN 30 '79			

Sons
and
Daughters
of
Mom

by Philip Wylie

Sons
and
Daughters
of
Mom

PHILIP WYLIE

DOUBLEDAY & COMPANY, INC., GARDEN CITY, NEW YORK
1971

Contents

Sons
and
Daughters
of
Mom

1. The People across the Chasm

This is a book about American youth.

It is a book about the Under-Thirties, the New People, Now People, the Revolutionaries and Rebels, the Activists and the Blacks, the New Left, the Hippies, the Cop-Outs and Dropouts, their Drug Scene, their Sex Revolution, their Reasonable Rage and Unreasonable, their Confrontations, Protests, Nonnegotiable Demands and strict Conventions.

It is a book about the other young people who are in the great majority and are generally known by the first sorts as squares. They were called, before President Nixon gave the term a wider meaning, the "silent majority."

Why did I write *another* book about this subject?

Haven't the militants cooled it anyhow?

Aren't America's young now largely engaged in a *constructive* attack on our polluted world?

Is there anything left to be said?

Obviously, I think there is.

Their curious and self-inflicted apartheid, the generation gap, by which the under-thirty people have cut off com-

munication with the rest of us, remains wide and perplexing
and as dangerous as it is artificial.

Most of us who are older by a decade or by several
decades still find many young Americans incomprehensible
even though most of them are equally enraged at the activist
minority.

Whether or not great and worse violences break out on
campuses and in city parks and streets, those that occurred
have left unanswered questions.

Why are the rebels so furious? Why is there so little communication across the arbitrary barrier of age thirty? Why
are so many so outraged by the experience of higher education? Why didn't the faculties and administrators foresee
what was to come? Why couldn't they manage the troubles
before they involved masses of other, usually silent, square
students? What did the turmoil achieve, if anything? And if
there was achievement, what is its nature?

Those are some residual questions and they will stand for
a long time and until answers are found.

The "sons and daughters of mom" about whom I write are
not only the revolutionary young people but many are
amongst the squarest. With them, too, whoever they are and
whatever their position in relation to the American establishment and system, something is wrong. This book is about
that wrong something.

As the fire-fuse carried explosions across the continent the
compulsion to write this book became so strong that I interrupted another effort, a work of fiction long in gestation,
to do so.

My compulsion had a force of several different kinds, all
driving me in the same direction.

One element was my philosophy, which is centered in the
young generation and all young generations. That will be
explained in the pages to follow.

Another part of it rose from my conviction that nobody was right in the turmoil, not the young and certainly not the adult majority who are but growing savagely vengeful.

A third was my sense, prevalent in all my years, that the reason for much of the rage, for the ineptitude with which its manifestations amongst students was met, and for the desperate, last-ditch acceptance by leaders among the under-thirty mutineers of nihilism, was a sheer will to destroy, an ideology of irrationalism.

That sense will be explained here, beginning with the next chapter.

Finally, as I shall note again in these pages, I had, or felt I had, a means of relating to the under-thirties.

About when the first members of that multitude were born, those now barely under thirty, I wrote another book which was a no-holds-barred assault on the same people they have attacked, the men and women who are now their parents, and everybody else in that generation.

The people the rebels will not even talk to, now, those who compose the hated establishment and run the loathed system, I called a "generation of vipers," in a book with that title.

In it, I made every criticism and criminal charge that young America is making now. I was, in that sense, their contemporary, thirty years ago. My age now may exile me from them by their mandatory statute of limitation.

But I hope not.

This book is meant for readers of all ages.

Baffled older readers may find in it some insights into the causes of the revolt of youth. And readers in the revolutionary ages, participants, activists or merely observers, sympathetic or hostile, may find that in other terms, too.

For, surely, a man who has had the anger of those furious under-thirties and for the same causes, since a time before

they were born and until this day, has some claim to young
attention. It may only be one of curiosity. The fact that I've
had those years to contemplate their state might be of interest,
though it comes from the side of the generation gap they
usually will not hear.

I hope that will not prevail amongst them in my case.

But I somewhat doubt they will receive this book with the
grace, the enthusiasm and the fascination that their parents
received that other, old diatribe against them, as vipers. For
in this book there are some harsh criticisms of young people,
some of whose ideas and acts I find as open to reproach as
they find ours.

And I sense that this new generation does not much listen
to criticism.

What most concerns me in the conflict of young against
old is the alienation felt by youth and the resulting quest
for identity.

To be without identity is to be without humanity.

But many young people search for a "new" identity by which
they mean a sense of self that will be new because it will be
opposite to what the seekers imagine the "identity" of the
enemy, "people over thirty."

There are so many fallacies in such assumptions that it is
difficult to take them seriously.

People who are under thirty and yet lump together all who
are older, for example, exhibit incompetence for any identity-
search. Identity involves individuality. The generalization
about their elders which regards them as all-one and all-
wrong is possible only to persons who see their younger mob
in the same way. And, of course, they do so see themselves.
Hair, costumes, common causes and mob behavior mark them
as the most regimented and least individuated generation
ever to appear.

The arbitrary selection of age thirty as the cut-off point is,

again, as absurd as mistaken. Nothing whatever *happens* to
any person, let alone, to all, on a thirtieth birthday. Even
as a symbol, the number has no meaning. How could it
apply to one who did not know his or her date of birth?
What imaginable physical or psychological shift occurs at
thirty? And what of themselves when they pass beyond that
dire date? Are they lost?

Or do they imagine the new identity they are only seeking
will be found in time to save them from the age of utter
ignominy? If so, they had better accelerate their quest with
every passing hour.

Again, presuming the identities of older people as utterly
misshapen and completely foul is stupid. Assuming the works
of everybody over thirty as worthless if not diabolic is preposterous. The radicals and others who take such blanket
views are not nearly as "bright" as they claim and as some
peculiar surveys seem to show. It is quite easy to prove that.

Suppose the absolutist antagonists of the establishment and
system were prohibited from using even a few of its artifacts?
Suppose, say, the under-thirty bank-burners were deprived of
the use of cars, planes, p.a. systems, amplifiers for musical
instruments, antibiotics, sulfa drugs, vaccines and local an-
aesthetics, to name a small number of contributions of people
over thirty? Without even those few their assemblies and
rock festivals would not be feasible and their filthy-mass-
revels would, if still attempted, end in epidemics.

So, while I share their detestation for many, many attitudes
of many older Americans I find their uncompromising damna-
tion both infantile and hypocritical. For they are also the
people who demand justice. The degree of injustice illustrated above becomes an index of their bigotry.

As bigots, they are unable even to search for identity. For
any acceptable identity-guest starts with honesty and its use
to find what is real and true. But where reality is deliberately

distorted or denied there can be no path to self-knowledge. What we see here is actually a passionate attempt to evade identity.

In a way, I am chagrined at not foreseeing the explosions of youth before they occurred. Who did? Among the hundreds of articles, reports, newspaper and magazine surveys, TV programs and the scores of books about the revolutionary young that I have consumed, studied or read, there was only *one* acknowledgment, by a professor, of the fact that he and his colleagues *ought* to have foreseen what was about to happen.

But even he did not have any sense of the impending revolt. He merely noted that people like himself who were closest to the young should have expected the blowup.

I should, and I have less excuse for failure.

My interest in young people has led me to keep in constant touch with a great many, both in and out of school. And there was a period before the thunder rolled when I tried to find the reason for a behavior pattern of students now forgotten. They were then called "the silent generation" and before that, "the beat generation."

In both periods their refusal to become involved in anything, their absence of reaction, their inertia and quietude perplexed adults. It was baffling—but it went unexplained.

I found the explanation. It was owing to the feeling among students that older persons, parents, faculty members and every adult "squelched them." None of them would listen to the students' ideas, consider their opinions, or even answer their questions. The adult world treated them as unworthy of interest. Professors were occupied, outside of the lecture hall, with other matters than human relations and communication with students. Parents put them down. So the rebelliousness against status quo that is normal in young people was compressed by that monstrous rejection. Even in the colleges and universities where meetings of a few students with top professors had been customary, such classes tended to disappear. Young and callow instructors increasingly replaced interesting professors. And, often, the rapid rise in student numbers, the "classroom load," made professor-student dialogues, if not impossible, at least too demanding on the best professors to continue.

The fuse, then, was alight. The pressure was building and it was palpable. Students knew that they were being belittled, avoided, dismissed as having no problems or ideas worth discussion, squelched, in their word that I heard over and over.

That "beat" and "silent" behavior was noted, but only with perplexity.

Before the explosions, I, at least, was no longer baffled. I knew about the pressure rising in the silence. But I missed its purport.

Even so, I am not sure that a change of adult-student relationships would have done more than delay the wrath. For I think that even if the faculties had managed to listen to and talk with these demeaned and segregated students, they would not have had the answers demanded.

The parents would not have had them, either.

They would not be found, and do not exist in the establishment, obviously.

So it is probable that the circumstances which kept the young silent but hotting-up would not have changed that, even if they'd been allowed a dialogue they were not.

What follows is an effort to explain both sides and, each to the other, to suggest what neither had or has, to exchange.

The problem is one of identity, of the *mistaken identity of everybody, irrespective of age.*

2. The Liberal Intellectual Establishment, or LIE

Most of the people under thirty who actively oppose what *they* call "The Establishment" and "The System" together with their sympathizers and those instructors and professors of whatever age who join or at least encourage the rebels, are unaware that they, too, are the products (and the dupes) of a different establishment and system. As liberal-intellectuals they see only the other power structure that, currently, is presumed in command in the nation.

By thinking of themselves as liberals and as people of intellect they create delusions. They seem to be apart from systems and managements such as the one they oppose. On that account, and since most of those who will be first to read this book will have that concept of themselves—literary critics and commentators, opinion-molders, educated Americans and academicians—it is essential that they be given a chance to note their old illusions before others can be usefully described.

These men and women, like the student rebels, consider themselves as an elite. Their academic background will have been in the arts, the humanities, in sociology, history, economics, political science and philosophy. If they are old, they may have been ardent advocates of the Old Left, and, probably, were sympathizers with that discredited group. If young, they will tend to call themselves a New Left. What they ignore is this:

The American Liberal Intellectual Establishment to which they belong has been mistaken in its every major view for the past half century.

Its members are, today, as deluded as before.

This sad truth does not mean that conservative Americans, people on the "right," were or are in any fashion more nearly correct in their ideas and their responses to events. They were and are not. If the evidence to follow seems to give aid and comfort to conventional people, that seeming will not last long.

However, liberal-intellectual readers who can bear to contemplate the record of their blunders may be able to see why the "establishment" and power structure they faulted, faulted them, and with cause. Intellectuals at least profess a capacity to understand facts that are historic; and as they follow a chronology of errors made by their sort, they ought to sense, finally, what it was, and is, about their "idealism" and their "humanitarianism," that stuck in the gorges of those others, the conservative, or "elite" power-establishment.

Consider, then, the ensuing sketch of realities and of the widespread or often universal attitudes and proposals of the LIE (Liberal Intellectual Establishment) at the same times:

1918–1923

The First World War was ended. Wilson's League of Nations was formed. Kerensky, the Wilson-supported premier of Russia, was driven from power and the Bolsheviks took over the Russian People's Revolution.

This era was dear to the heart of America's LIE. It believed that peace could be made eternal. It supported the con-

ferences that led to arms limitations. It denied any worried
claim that the dicing up of Europe by France, England and
America was folly and would lead to a next war. It was
bemused with the Russian Revolution and also with the violent strife of American labor against management. Not yet
truly leftist, the liberal-intellectuals were, in this period, left-
fascinated, pro-labor, smugly pacifist and profoundly happy
in their effectiveness, under Wilson, as the bringers of eternal
peace.

On November 8–9 of 1923, Hitler led the so-called Beer
Hall Putsch. He was a ridiculous fool in the LIE view, who
was jailed after the abortive putsch and who then began to
write a book. The LIE scarcely noticed and when it did, it
laughed.

1926

A certain Dr. Robert H. Goddard flew the first liquid-fuel
rocket and his extrapolations (with proofs) foretold the future
of that new system. The LIE skipped what little press mention there was of Goddard's work.

At Locarno, Germany was admitted to the League of Nations. The LIE hailed it as another guarantee of their belief
in lasting peace.

1929

Many liberals and intellectuals had joined in the Great
Boom of the twenties and become wealthy—on paper. They
had enjoyed the excitements of the "Jazz Age," the "Golden"
or "Roaring Twenties." In New York City, Chicago, and in
some other centers, the liberals and intellectuals had righteously joined the rest of the nation's leaders in violating the
Volstead Act, and so, in abetting the rise of gangsterism, a
dramatic spin-off which the LIE regarded as incidental, and
as mere material for literary work. In preceding years Paris
had been the LIE Mecca; and the new art forms were a LIE
rage: Dada, impressionism, cubism, futurism and stream-of-

consciousness arts. James Joyce was hailed as the greatest
innovator and topmost living genius of letters, equal to or
surpassing Shakespeare. Thus, a growing reverence for experimental prose and poetry and for nonrepresentational art
took root.

The stock market crash on October 29 was the tocsin of
the Great Depression that lay ahead.

Before the year was out many briefly rich leaders among
the intellectuals and liberals were penniless or left with their
small salaries as professors, editors, critics and so on. The
stage was set for new LIE postures soon to develop.

1930

The London Naval Reduction Treaty was signed by Brit-
ain, the USA, and Japan—a feat the LIE saw as a next
guarantee of the goal they had so long even advertised in
the media, under the aegis of what they had called "World
Peaceways."

1931

America was deep in the Depression.
Japan overran Manchuria.

1933

Roosevelt gave diplomatic recognition to the USSR. The
liberal-intellectuals by now had seen the "infamous" nature
of capitalism and were beginning to align themselves seriously
with the Marxists. Soviet recognition was their idea of a
great leap forward for freedom, peace and progress. Their
"man" was in the White House and they, as his "brain trust,"
were soon to become all-powerful.

As this year began, however, Hitler became chancellor of
Germany (January 30). In May, the Republican government
of Spain disenfranchised the Roman Catholic Church, also a
LIE win. In October, Germany quit the League of Nations
and withdrew from the disarmament talks.

1934
Dollfuss, chancellor of Austria, assassinated by Nazis.
1935
Hitler rejected the Versailles Treaty and ordered conscription.

Italy invaded Ethiopia. The League of Nations invoked sanctions against the aggressor. The LIE was outraged at Mussolini.

1936
Hitler reoccupied the Rhineland.

Franco entered Spain to put down the Republican government.

Italy annexed Ethiopia.

Japan and Germany signed an "anti-Comintern" pact.

The liberal-intellectuals of the United States were, by now, often ardently and openly pro-Soviet. Many of their leaders joyously visited the USSR and most came back full of admiration and praise in which there was little adverse finding and much great expectation. The LIE was also working in the labor movement. A Communist party of considerable size arose in USA and the LIE widely tended to support it, or, minimally, its alleged aims and ideals.

The "century of the common man" was born in USA, child of the LIE, and "common man" was seen as akin to Marx's "economic man."

The pro-Communist American liberal-intellectual tourists in the USSR were not capable of seeing that Soviet industry was a serf-mill and shambles or that the collective farms were cruel and wasteful. They had no notion (as other non-LIE visitors in the USSR did have) that Stalin's infamous purges had begun.

1937–1939
In this period, the first and for a long time the major concern of the LIE was the war in Spain. Many young members

of the cult gave their lives in the struggle, fighting with the Soviet interventionists against Franco and his Italian and German cohorts. Few such partisans gained any insight into the tyrannical nature of Stalinism. Hemingway was an exception of sorts.

In these years, then, the LIE position was "pro-freedom," as in its stand for Republican Spain. No thought was given, then or ever, to the alternative fate, if the Republicans had withstood Franco, and so, Spain had fallen under the thrall of Stalin.

Japan's rape of China also marked the era. The LIE deplored it.

Two major citizen's committees were formed in USA, one to urge isolation; it was called "America First." The other, called "The Committee to Defend America by Aiding the Allies," had as its slogan "Stop Hitler." It appealed to some liberal-intellectuals but was too militant for many. Their faith in and fascination with the USSR was so intense (and the residual hopes of the LIE for enduring peace were so strong, still) that even the betrayal of Czechoslovakia by England's Chamberlain was widely seen as but a topic for bitter talk by the LIE.

Spain's Republic fell in March 1939.

The LIE was ecstatic when Mexico nationalized its oil industry in March.

Roosevelt had "asked" Hitler to keep the peace, in October, in 1938. He kept asking.

On January 22, 1939, at Columbia University, the atom was "split." The LIE didn't even know what that meant.

What did happen, on August 24, 1939, that revealed their now-long folly to many members of the LIE was the signing of a ten-year nonaggression pact by Stalin and Hitler.

The LIE-humiliating Finnish-USSR war ended in March. But in July, the USSR annexed the Baltic States.

1941

On December 7 the Japanese attacked Pearl Harbor. This assault by Japan was not expected in the LIE or among most others. The USA was forced into World War II.

By this time, many main concepts, aims, fealties and postures of the LIE had been discredited.

The liberal-intellectual fixation on peace had led to disarmament. America was unready for war largely owing to LIE advocacy and its implementation. The liberal-intellectual view of the USSR had proven a sickening blunder. That both the Nazi and Red forms of government were absolutist and sustained by terror had long been known; but the LIE remained pro-USSR and only mildly, in effect, anti-Hitler, until those poses were revealed, temporarily, for them, as madness, mere wishes with no support.

For the first year after Pearl Harbor the USA remained in a condition of apathy. A people who had wanted no part of any war, and who had been induced to expect peace during twenty years and more by the intellectual and liberal leaders of American thought, was now at war, and naked of weapons. The liberal-intellectual government, Roosevelt and his brain trust, would not even reveal the nature of the enemy, keeping secret such horrors as the Bataan March. They believed the American people would and must wage war, not in anger, but according to LIE abstractions and so-called ideals. This folly, this federal policy for a year, was surely responsible for the expensive apathy of that period.

The absence of realism, the overweening and self-righteous posture of the LIE thus came close to costing USA its existence.

1945

The Nazi horde was beaten. In August, after USA dropped two A-bombs on two cities, Japan also gave up. The Atomic

Age arrived. From August 6 on, it was not possible to think usefully about any broad human problem unless one had a good understanding of nuclear physics and of biology. There was no such knowledge in the liberal-intellectual establishment and there came to be very little in the years that followed.

If, in fact, the LIE had understood biology enough to know what biologists knew of man it would have found, before the Second World War, that Marxism was wrong in so basic a way as to invalidate the Communist Faith. Genetics showed that.

In the years between 1918—when World War I ended, and those after V-E and V-J Days silenced World War II—in, say, that third of a century, America's liberals and intellectuals were that widely and that often near-unanimously wrong. Their striving for peace may have been noble in aim but the effort brought America to the edge of disaster. Their sympathy with the USSR, and/or Marxism, was totally wrong and more than once revealed, not as "treasonable," which the masses and many congressmen thought, but as proof of their intellectual incapacity and their incomprehension of the nature of reality and freedom.

They did not think. They were not knowledgeable. Relevance and reason were not accessible to them because of their ignorance.

They espoused the rebel cause in Spain but they could not see that a rebel victory would mean one more Hungary or Czechoslovakia on the Iberian Peninsula.

They failed to dream of what was to be the ultimate result of Japan's rampage in China. The effect of their "idealism" and of the profiting industrialist's pacifism induced a year of apathy after the "day of infamy." The LIE never saw its errors.

It blamed all wartime troubles and all prior economic calamity on "malefactors of great wealth" or "fascists," their targets still.

The alleged malefactors responded by trying to show that Roosevelt "got us into war" through somehow staging the giant and ignominious calamity at Hawaii, equally mad!

The LIE support of "labor" was idealist, plainly. Or was it? Was the present reality foreseen? Is labor's power over management ideal? Is it noble of unions to erase newspapers, price their members out of work and escalate inflation? And what is or was intelligent or liberal in the support of organized millions who were and remain *racist*, an alleged LIE abomination and a nation-wide injustice? How extremist, how blind, how perfidious and how prejudiced can one be and still claim virtue or reasonableness?

If there were two of me and the other were a scholar he perhaps could and would search out the hundred thousand major documents (conservatively!) which, read now, would firm up this abbreviated case against the liberal-intellectuals. One could quote from their mountains of books, their radio speeches and public addresses, their columns and editorials and the ten thousand magazine pieces they published, to show exactly and in detail their massive and constant errors in belief, in concept, in appraisals, value judgments and predictions. One could display their massive ignorance, as easily.

3. Proof of the Puddingheads

People under thirty will not, of course, have any personal recollection of the grim, incessant default of the generation of intellectuals and liberals who steadily led America into Nowheresville in the years before they were born. If they are now unwilling to read the record or if they read it as it has been so widely blurred, altered, or skipped, in such textbooks and histories as they are usually given (works of members of the academic or academy-oriented LIE), they will not have any basis for judging contemporary ideas as they are revealed fallacious by the old, liberal-intellectual version of what the new versions present, still, as true.

It would not be possible for a man or woman with a fair mind and a sense of reality to belong to something called the New Left if the history of the Old Left were understood. And it is not possible for any self-respecting (let alone, respected) person to *be* the former or *merit* the latter, if his public utterance by mouth or in writing reveals he lacks the information basic for cogent reflection on man.

How gruesome the errors of people without needed knowledge can be, is shown by a final American disaster in which all liberals and all intellectuals of every hue (or of complete pallor) took part. Owing to ignorance, America, in the years immediately after the Second World War, lost its most precious, its only indispensable possession.

What the United States lost then was its freedom.

Access to knowledge must be total. Where plain knowledge of any sort is concealed from a people, they will no longer have freedom and so will not be able to govern themselves. Even if they do not know how much knowledge, of what sort, in what areas, is being withheld from them, they will not be free. When any government is able, even, to mark some bit of pure knowledge "secret," that government becomes a tyranny and a tyranny of a scope, sort and threat the public will not even be able to judge.

In the United States, prior to World War II, there had always been a small amount of this unfree hocus-pocus. It was called "military secrecy" but then it concerned only a few *applications* of scientific theory and did not and could not—to the distress of Pentagon-minded men—halt or even compromise the free exchange of pure scientific *knowledge* amongst all scholars in the world, save for those in Red or Fascist nations.

Pure knowledge was still absolutely free and open to all.

Presumably, at least, any person who called himself both liberal and an intellectual, any author, politician, professor, lecturer or other such citizen, would acknowledge that the right to all knowledge is basic to liberty and essential for self-government.

However, after the Second World War the problem of maintaining the public right to know became crucial.

What America was then obliged to do to remain a free and self-governed land was the issue. For, now, suddenly, we had entered the Atomic Age and either we had to make access to that scientific knowledge open to all or we had to stamp it *secret* . . . and cease being a free people.

The crisis was precisely that simple and of exactly that dramatic nature. America flunked.

4. The LIE: Collegiate Gothic

What is amusingly called "higher education" was designed
in the Dark Ages by monks to maintain the dark forever.
The aim of the college was religious in those centuries and
only slowly broadened to include a somewhat secular instruction in philosophies other than the Catholic and finally
the Protestant. Reading Latin was always necessary but undergraduates had to cover their heads and their lit candles
to peruse Horace or Ovid.

Other subjects crept into the curriculum. History, of course,
was an early one—and history was, as now, only the special
lies that present a national past of an uplifting nature,
skimping or omitting any of the country's mistakes such as
its centuries of ruthlessness, its bigotry, its inquisitions, lost
wars, usuries, battles motivated by gain, oppressions, slaveries,
genocide, the wringing out of lesser breeds of every tangible
coin, mass panics and political errors and the portions of
the lives of great men that were less than that, by going
moral standards or even by real and ethical criteria.

Thus the so-called Puritan ethic came to America and
academe was at first godly to the core even though it slowly

offered past generations a degree in what it came to call
the "liberal arts." A graduate in the liberal arts or in the
"arts and humanities" was presumed as educated as could
be managed and was that, in the academic certainty, right
into the twentieth century.

Early in that age some colleges and universities grudgingly
recognized the existence of science. A very few. Cornell,
for a rare example, renamed the major category of learning
"arts and sciences" but most students of the arts, the liberal
arts and the humanities are still made to concentrate on
matter in those earlier categories. A mandatory freshman
course in one science became fairly fashionable in the twenties,
but which one, was a student choice and, left to their own
options, students, already full of fury at education, generally
ineducable owing to prior schooling and aware that science
was difficult, usually accepted whatever branch of that area
of search and knowledge was known to be easiest in their
given institution.

Till recently, two semesters of geology, for example, would
constitute the scientific background of a Bachelor of Arts, an
M.A. in Sociology or a Ph.D. in Education, itself! But contemporary students widely hold all science "irrelevant."

The grisly result caused me to point out, elsewhere, that
contemporary man is relatively the most ignorant in the history
of his species. That is a fact and the catastrophic proofs are
just beginning to appear. Let me make that situation so clear
that even A.B.'s can understand it.

Pure science is knowledge and only knowledge, including
the knowledge of ways to add to or alter the whole. It is
also called "natural science" and it has set forth the principal
concepts and laws that now serve to define the universe.
These are the laws of physics and chemistry, operable and
immutable from the beginning of the cosmos and their corollaries, the laws of biology, which took effect when life arose

and have been operational (as well as inviolable) ever since. Not to know them is to be unable to think or act sanely in this era.

The stuff that the LIE calls "knowledge" consists of what people theorize about people but "people" as if they were apart from nature and not subject to the laws of physics, chemistry or biology. Art and letters, history, philosophy, religion, theology, political and social "science," economics, law, business, including salesmanship, advertising and managment, even (again) *education itself*—the whole learning-bag of the LIE—is in essence a mythology. With little or more often no reference to people as merely one species dwelling in nature and as subject to the laws of nature as salamanders and bacteria, it can be only myth.

The predicament of existence by fables is now dawning on the dis-educated swarms of the LIE in a dim, vague and vulgar fashion. Amidst our thickening smog, beside our polluted waters and on our poisoned land the LIE-indoctrinated majority has reacted to its discomfort. But the degree of that reaction is on the order of one thousandth of 1 percent of the appropriate, that is, the necessary sort. Even social and political "scientists" are commencing to be nervous about our pathological landscape and the "population explosion."

The latter is generally seen as an event taking place elsewhere and the former is mostly regarded as if it were a cosmetic problem and one, furthermore, which could be remedied by added technological gimmickry. Man's actual place as an animal in nature is unseen. Unknown are the laws that cannot and never could be violated without penalties often a million times more severe than seems "fair" to people educated exclusively by people-about-people "studies." But no member of the LIE is qualified for useful thought.

If that seems exaggerated, the seeming will serve excellently as a gauge of the reader's stupidity. And that, too, is readily demonstrated as to scale. For if the people in this allegedly well-educated land had a real education they would have been engaged, long before this moment, in that one ecological endeavor they haven't even noted. They would have appropriated tens of billions and, long since, embarked on the step that must first be taken if man is even to try to survive. They would be financing myriads of scientists in an all-out, cost-no-object attempt to discover how badly off the planet's biosphere and its numberless eco-systems *already are.*

Until that situation is as thoroughly researched and learned as well as can be managed by appropriate scientists in the relevant disciplines (and that is all the hundreds of fields in the natural sciences) we cannot even establish priorities for what to do (or undo) in what order. Until that massive, world-wide effort is undertaken *and completed* not one man or woman or child will even be able to make an "educated *guess*" about the mere possibility of human survival.

For all any scientist knows, and for all the lot of them know, we may already have done, in our world environment, some single act, (or even many dozen acts), that cannot be reversed yet will spell the doom of mankind. Only when and if we learn, to the best ability of the best qualified people, that we seem to have, still, a chance to survive can we arrange steps toward salvation in a rational order. At this writing, however, there is no sign that Americans have education enough, that is, knowledge enough, to imagine the nature of the mandatory beginning of what then might be an opportunity to proceed toward human survival.

It is the radical under-thirty people who assert science is irrelevant. These second generation vipers are, of course, the offspring of liberal, intellectual (and affluent) parents. Their posture is a reaction to the illusion that what they deplore, the world of the over-thirties, *is* scientific . . . and *rational!* Thus they reveal themselves as doubly mindless, the most excessive underachievement of mankind to date.

What is science? Knowledge and a method that requires complete open-mindedness and perfect honesty. It is an objective discipline, then. The scientist observes a chosen phenomenon, measures and describes it, and if some notion of a new relationship or any other novel but sensible-seeming aspect of his phenomenon occurs to him, he designs experiments to test his hunch. Or he reverses that order, theorizing first and then experimenting to check. If his work seems sound he publishes the results in a journal read by associates in his special field. They, then, repeat the experiment to test the data first, and either confirm or disprove the man's proposition. When it is confirmed, that man or woman will have made a contribution to science. But, even then, whatever new concept or datum he has disclosed will be held open to modification, alteration, even rejection, if some clearer or broader proven theory requires that.

Thus science ideally is an unfinished business, progress in processes that have no final resolution. Of course, many "facts" are acceptable as fact, such as the movement of the earth around the sun or the bacterial and then the viral causation of disease. So there does exist a massive, ever-growing body of sure knowledge, knowledge that can be accepted by men of all nations and races, speaking all languages, in complete agreement. Even though all this "truth" may present further questions to the scientist, he has a definite basis from which to seek answers to more delicate or remote questions. He knows about this rotation of the earth and its revolution, too. He is still, however, uncertain of the causes of wobble in the earth as it spins on its axis. Again, he has measured earth's magnetic field but found its poles reverse at long intervals, a matter not yet understood.

To a liberal-intellectual, however, it was not the information science rapidly elicited that seemed important but the enviable efficacy of the method. He was, say, a professor of literature, and there, a specialist in political essayists, or perhaps his metier was aesthetics. Everything in his field and in the liberal arts and humanities had been, till this moment, discursive, theoretical, open to contention and without any such basis as was seen in science.

So he began to "apply," as he imagined it, "scientific methodology" to his interests. Early in this century, as this author and many others have pointed out, the liberal arts and humanities bloomed with alleged sciences, political science, social sciences, scientific laws of economics, and all these, of course, were rooted in the science of behaviorism which subtended and largely still underlies pedagogy.

It is not possible to have a science of sociology or any of the other sorts noted, along with those implied, because the phenomenon involved is man, as an individual and in groups and masses. If man's psychology, his nature, motivation, relationship to all nature and all his subjective processes were understood thoroughly, then, but only then, a political or a social science might be feasible, and economic laws of validity could perhaps be adduced. Since, however, conditioned reflex theory, and the theory of operant conditioning have failed completely to explain a massive amount of the behavior of rats and deer, moose, pigs and men, the grounds for these alleged sciences simply do not exist.

But the LIE, academic wing, rushed into the development and teaching of multitudes of such fishy fantasies in the conviction that, now, great areas of the liberal arts and especially of the humanities were truly sciences. Undergraduates and graduate students, having no sufficient access to real science and thus, no understanding of the real method of its discipline, not surprisingly assumed that what they were then taught about society, the market, trade, government, nations, political action, trends and mass-movements furnished a statistical "predictability for human affairs and was, therefore, scientific.

This nefarious business has gone forward for more than a half century now. It is directly responsible for the failure of the liberal-intellectual leadership in America. It is the reason the great majority of Americans who believe themselves to be educated and have bachelors' degrees, M.A.'s and Ph.D.'s to prove it, are, in fact, so ignorant of the means to and the state of hard knowledge as to be intellectually infantile. They are not scientists, of course. The fact that many actual scientists are liberals, while true enough in a way, has little meaning here, since their liberalism will usually be some generous but unscrutinized version of or accord with the position of the LIE.

The result has been seen as "two cultures" the scientist-liberal, C. P. Snow, discussed. The term, as widely used, is erroneous. Neither is a "culture"; but one has a solid base; the other, not. A genuine culture has never existed nor has half of one.

Among scientists much puzzlement rises from the failure of the ordinary citizen to comprehend relevant information and make its sure inferences. Among the overwhelmingly larger body of nonscientific but allegedly educated people, including the ranks of liberal-intellectual establishment in our colleges and universities and those in the world beyond such narrow precincts, millions of men and women who believe they are educated, the situation is seen differently, if at all.

Here, the *other* "establishment and system," the one students so facilely assault and decry, is the goat. The "power structure," "big government and its bureaucracy" and the "military-industrial complex" are held to be the source and cause of man's innumerable difficulties. There is a general

failure in every "technological society" to apply the whole
of scientific knowledge to the human condition and not just
that part which increases wealth, swells the gross national
product, supplies arms, provides added services and, so, im-
proves the economic estate of everybody. That failure, hazily
perceived by the LIE, is blamed on the establishment and
system, at least in the United States. The indentical failure in
Red nations is not noted the same way.

To the most observant and knowledgeable economist, social
or political scientist, humanist, intellectual and liberal, there
is always a target group with an attached name; and that
group, its management and the system it uses, is the supposed
cause of the present and crucial problem: what we have
that is being fabricated, distributed and serviced in ways
which are destroying the environment.

The scientists who see that dilemma feel to some degree
that it is their own fault, owing to their failure in communicating what they have learned and know, and the implications
of that whole. They are correct to a degree. But there they
tend to imagine the average man as a being with a mind
and an available capability for reason, a capacity for logic,
like their own, or, rather, like their own minds as these
will have been used in one or more of their hundreds of
special fields. Thus their sense of the possibility of change
and betterment by communication is exaggerated. They seem
nearly unaware of the forces of resistance in the public masses
which have no adequate schooling for understanding science,
in any case. And they are almost equally blind to the fact
that, as educated men, they are vastly outnumbered by
others with an education assumed as high as theirs and
usually higher, by virtue of its being "broader" than the training of those who are merely doctors in biology or in bio-
chemistry or astrophysics.

This great overwhelming majority of educated men and

women will in effect be a-scientific, or even worse, it will
be composed of individuals who imagine their social and political science and their knowledge of economic laws makes
them more capable of social and cultural planning than any
exact or pure scientist, and, of course, any mere applied
scientist. This is a huge class of dominant people who, in
fact, will have no training in reality, but only mistraining
by liberal-intellectuals whose "reality" is people-fast.

It is true that scientific knowledge has not been communicated, as proven data, or as a basis for prediction (of the
most menacing sorts), to the public.

That it has not been communicated to the majority of
supposedly educated men—leaders, now, in nearly every
major area of life from politics to business management,
from social planning to all professions save the genuinely
scientific—is also evident.

But the idea that the problems of our technological society
can be resolved and our imminent perils avoided by changing the present establishment and system—which is the
widespread conviction of conscious conservatives and liberal-
intellectuals, so, the overwhelming certainty of rebellious
youth—is false. The fallacy isn't visible to the very people who
think they understand society best. It is less than visible
to the young leftists and mutineers, a quantum they will
call propaganda if they ever detect its presence.

Neither the scientist, however liberal, nor the great bulk
of nonscientific but allegedly educated men who are vocal
and who lead in forming opinion, here, are aware of the
real cause of the dilemma, which is *all people,* themselves
included.

As the earth dies, the responsibility lies not with the
present system or any imaginable replacement of that. To
accuse the military-industrial or corporate management of
that or of any related dilemma is simple-minded. The blame

rests on what people want and get, including all consumers
of all goods and all users of all services everywhere, technological or social.

It is true, as Galbraith noted, that industry must try to
determine what will "sell" in years ahead at a point five or
ten years from any present. It is also true that the mass of
what is then made in mock-up and arranged for fabrication
by retooling is usually marketed profitably after its manufac-
ture. Advertising, on TV and in all other media, achieves
that. But no human being is obliged even to look at TV
or read or listen to advertising on or in other media. Nobody
is compelled to purchase what industry had preplanned,
made and later offers for sale. The further fact that industry,
in this programming of what it will make, shrewdly studies
what the public will likely want, or be susceptible of being
induced to imagine it wants, and so, will buy, in no way
removes the onus from the population. That industry can
anticipate or even fabricate greed amongst two hundred millions of people does not alter the fact that greed is the basic
factor, present greed and greed that is only waiting to be
triggered.

An identical greed motivates people under Marxist establishments and systems.

Again, the immensity of our military establishment and
its production is not owing to military power but to a national
illusion and a national fear of something America calls "Communism," which, as a recent poll showed, not quite two
American adults in a hundred can define.

Thus nearly all Americans oppose what few understand, so
that efforts most deem "anti-Communist" are as likely to
assist actual Red endeavors as to blunt them—a result
evident in rightist ploys and in the tyrannical, freedom-kill-
ing efforts or un-American committees and their endeavors.
The intense fear of this actually unknown demon called

Communism has very largely diverted general attention to
false and idiotic suspicion of honorable and free and generally
intelligent people while it has kept the great American majority from seeing it is hanging itself. Our very trust in
American "power" is as absurd, since its maximum use will
be suicidal.

Again, the Vietnam war is immoral and has been, from
our first interest in what was a just-liberated French colony.
But the frantic cries of immorality leveled against the
nasty situation in recent years have not referred to the
really immoral behavior of the United States in that crime.
Instead, they are largely plaints based on infantile points,
points irrelevant, silly and trivial compared to the vastness
of our actual wrongdoing. Yet they also characterize the LIE
style of "thinking."

John F. Kennedy certainly had the best and most up-to-
date education of any American President and he was liberal
as well. One of the most covertly powerful men in the nation
was the late Cardinal Spellman. Kennedy began to escalate
our alliance with the Vietnamese military-business-Roman
Catholic-French speaking power structure, a totalitarian minority of oppressors of the majority, after Spellman's missions
to that miserable nation. America thereby augmented its
support of a new tyranny over self-freed colonials who were
the vast majority.

It will not, hopefully, be necessary to continue endlessly
with such instances of errors of educated, liberal establishments and their top people. Roosevelt probably made the
most and worst miscalculations and he was next-best educated to JFK, the other darling of the LIE.

One added trifle might be useful, though.

John F. Kennedy made a grim error in certain ad-libbed
evaluations of Soviet weapons experiments. This author wrote

the President, a man he admired despite his just-cited and evil error, and has the President's letter of thanks for the correction—to which may be added the historical fact that JFK never again made a similar lapse in public statements about nuclear matters, about which he had proven himself ignorant to a degree frightening in any man in the White House. So some liberals are sometimes somewhat educable.

The members of the LIE are considered to be, personally, a very fine type of human being, as folks say. Their motives, far more often than those of any other category of person, are unselfish and even noble, in their minds.

Without their intercessions in critical instances involving the threat to the rights of individuals and minorities, America might now be some sort of corporate state and would be a worse shambles, at least, than its present shambles-in-progress.

What emerges from the record of the LIE, from countless failures, from the division of education into two uncultured categories and from the dominion of the academic world by the LIE (along with the desertion of many scientists to the ivory tower), is this:

Education itself has failed. Educators are not educated.

For fifty years pedagogical methods from primary through secondary and to college levels have been based on theoretical fallacies about man, his nature, nature itself and the learning process.

Very few individuals now entering colleges and universities are actually educable. Few have been, in the past half century and more. Nine-tenths of all college graduates in that long period have not been motivated to examine (let alone, keep up with) the major parts of knowledge that have been added to what mankind previously knew, theories and facts

that have changed the condition of man and that will go
on doing so but that the LIE is only vaguely and rather
patronizingly aware of, if at all.

The size of the American delusion about its educated state
and the increase of that deadly fraud cannot be exaggerated.

Not twenty men in our Senate and House of Representatives
have sufficient education to enable them to assess half of the
daily problems that are their concern. Not many more have
even enough knowledge to judge which experts will give
them accurate, complete and reliable information in the
myriad areas of their ignorance.

Hardly a voter in a thousand could learn enough, even if
America were free, to make an appropriate decision about
most of the issues or the capability of the candidates for
whom he votes.

America is no more a democracy or a republic than was
Babylon.

As my friend, the renowned anthropologist-psychologist
Gregory Bateson, said in a private communication, this
situation adds up to another: "Nobody's in charge."

"The men in charge . . . are not in charge."

They think, perhaps, they are in charge, as senators and
representatives, as a President and his Cabinet, as the heads
of industry, the top brass at the Pentagon, the faculties and
administrators of universities and colleges, teachers, engineers
and others.

They *think* they are in charge.

They give orders, get things done, vote, plan, produce
military hardware, turn out estimates of the GNP, "run" our
government and its bureaucracies, practice "statecraft" and
the like. We, the public, imagine that in electing those who
govern we manage ourselves. Educators think they were and
even are educating people enough for self-government and
whenever they are forced to notice our mass stupidities they

say that something is the matter with *people*, or with *communicating*, or with the Big System and Establishment, but almost never with their own concepts of pedagogy.

Never do they ask why so much education has resulted in such mass ignorance.

Never does it strike them that they who were supposedly in charge of education have failed to produce the real thing. Why?

Nobody is in charge, as Bateson states.

Nobody is, because even in this most "advanced" of all nations in all time, we have no way to make use of what is known by some few that affects all.

Nature is in charge, not man.

And nature forgives no trespasses or blunders.

I often think, as the rebel students keep demanding that their studies be made relevant, how right!

But it is an ironic reflection.

For—remember—the tens of thousands of leaders and activists among the undergraduate mutineers, along with all who sympathize with these New Left, SDS and other kindred boobs are, *almost to a single one, products or students of the liberal arts and humanities.*

Undergraduates aiming at scientific careers, even at careers in applied science, engineering, medicine and all such professions *except* "education," have no concern with these "revolutionary know-nothings.

The rebels are the people who clamor for "relevant" courses. But they make plain what sort of instruction they regard as without their absurd idea of relevance. Foremost in that list are the sciences and with them, technology. Next, of all incredible follies, they apparently consider history least relevant.

What remains is their curriculum of liberal arts and humanities, all they have had experience of, and it is irrelevant,

to be sure, but not the way they imagine. For their hatred
of our establishment and system is based on its technological
form and the "depersonalizing" or "alienating" effect of that.
To reject it on such ground is understandable in people who
cannot think and will not learn whatever they imagine is
the source of their woe, or somebody's. But rejection, rebellion and destruction, as sole social motives, can't serve. The
merely anti-youths are intent upon courses identical with
those pursued by Attila and Genghis Khan.

A vastly deeper and wider knowledge of science and
technology is essential for *any* change in the system and
establishment of any relevant sort, any sort that even hopefully might shift it toward the human values the destroyers
pretend to know and feign to promote.

Thus we see a rebellion against education that is, owing
to education, twice as wrong as it was in the Old Left. Nobody in America is as reactionary as these activists.

5. Materialism as Sin and Virtue

Money may not be the root of all evil but it certainly is the root, trunk and branch of most non-thought.

Capitalism is all about money.

Marxism is too.

"In general," said a young lady president of a chapter of Students for a Democratic Society in a large university, "I would say SDS agrees with the Marxist analysis."

In general, the New Left must agree with Marx's "analysis," to take that name.

But it is not possible for such people to agree with any Marxist "synthesis," instances of which are variously and highly visible in the many nations that are Communist. Even the most bald and far-out New Leftist must be aware that all these countries are police states, terror-governed, totalitarian, places where freedom of expression is taboo, thought and opinion are controlled and lands in which their own intransigence would, on first emergence, get them rushed to a Siberia or a grave.

They are leftist, then, only because they oppose what they

call the right. American materialism enrages them because
it is the fruit of capitalism.

Dialectical materialism does not even irk.

American materialism is, indeed, the result of the capitalist
system to a great extent and of government largess to a
lesser degree. It has produced a far higher incidence of
citizens with far more "economic power" than any other system anywhere.

The original "Marxist analysis," of course, passionately opposed capitalist exploitation of the worker and "peasant" as
it existed a century ago. Capitalism and its abuses could be
reversed, Marx believed, only when the exploited classes
rebelled and set up a new establishment and system. In this
new one, the state would own all the means of production
and all resources. These would be managed so that every
citizen got an even chance at his share of everything—goods,
services, education, medical aid and all.

Capitalism didn't furnish that equality of environment and
opportunity which the new system would supply. With it,
all men would rise to measureless heights since all men were
equal and only their unequal opportunity under monarchy
or capitalism kept most men torpid serfs, ignorant slaves,
exploited and helpless workers.

That part of the original Marxist "synthesis" was, of course,
Pavlovian. It made sense if the classical behaviorists made
sense. If men were born "blank slates" and were made what
they became afterward by environment alone, that is, by the
conditioning of their reflexes, and if no other factor was of
any moment in human nature, Marx was right.

It is funny, now, that anybody can be naive enough to
accept either the "Marxist analysis" or its projections. Few
theories have been so completely exploded.

Genetically, as has been noted, Marx was in error. Much
of what an individual is, perhaps most, and so, what he or

she becomes or does not become, is owing to inheritance. For decades the USSR tried to maintain the biological farce that this is not true. Stalin's "Lysenkoism," named for the biologist who tried to affirm the Marxist foolishness, caused rational biological research in the USSR to be impossible for decades and was the laughingstock of the free world.

The test of any theory is in its accuracy as prediction. There, too, Marxism has collapsed. The vast, terrible and true abuses of capitalism of Marx's era have vanished, except in Marxist nations. The worker, under capitalism, has a power often coequal with the owners and with management. Not the few but tens of millions of Americans own shares in corporations. Duress of the sort Marx beheld has disappeared in the capitalist society; but it has become far more prevalent and vicious under all systems of dialectical materialism.

One is therefore left baffled by any New Leftist who is able to imagine validity in that sort of dogma. Marx's thesis was based on a biological fallacy. His predictions have proven to be worse than mistaken, the very opposite of what he prophesied from his "law" has occurred.

That deity of the liberal-intellectuals of the thirties and forties, "economic man," has turned out to be other, too. His motives aren't what Marx thought since the collective state has not enabled man to keep anywhere near abreast, economically, even, with the capitalist nations.

The paradoxes and ironies only begin, there.

When Marx tried to dream up a better world he fantasied a world where serfs, peasants and mightily oppressed proletarians constituted the brains and muscle of production.

No American I ever heard of has called himself a peasant or allowed anyone to do so. None has accepted his status as proletarian. There had been black slaves in America and they were freed but their ensuing miseries had and have nothing to do with the Marxist concepts.

The era of the robber barons has long vanished.

What the New Left seems to desire is, in a sense, still, a "redistribution" of wealth. Like the Old Left, these people see the real tragedy of poverty in USA, slum horrors and black repression. Money spent or somehow issued to those who have the least, will solve all problems, they assume. Money, and of course, more education, which depends on more money.

It does not even occur to many that, however high the standard of living in America might rise, and even if it became sufficient and fairly enough "distributed" to provide everybody, black, white, whatever, with nice housing and an income on an electric-kitchen-one-car-traded-in-every-three-years standard, along with twelve or even sixteen years of what we consider "education," there would *still* be a group of, say, 10 per cent of all, who would be at the bottom of *that* heap. And that 10 per cent would, obviously, know that 90 per cent of its fellow citizens were "better off."

In other words, to imagine *any* extension of money, *any* universal economic gain that would remove *every* present criterion of poverty, every absence of "advantage," of "oppression" and "injustice," no matter how great it might be as a design of an acceptable utopia, is feeble-minded. There will always be economic gradations, even in the most completely affluent society conceivable. And as a result there will always be a considerable group who will be relative have-nots in their own and in everybody's eyes.

While this is not any indication that the level of misery, poverty and economic and social injustice of our present is acceptable, it does show that, to the degree that man is "economic man," he is insatiable. And it indicates very clearly that man isn't just "economic." He is motivated in many other ways such as a drive toward status, a will for power, a competitiveness with his fellows in areas far outside any economic "sufficiency," including many areas which cause the critics of American "materialism" to protest the effects of affluence on the existing masses that now have a fair amount!

Even the term "economic sufficiency" becomes absurd when seen in that light. What is it? Where is it? What American family believes that it has achieved "sufficiency" and wants nothing more than what it has? Who, on earth, save the very rich, if it be true of some few of them, has enough? What is the criterion of "enough" for a family of six, husband, wife and four children, ages ten to twenty? Will a net annual income of fifteen thousand dollars a year, of thirty, seem economically a "sufficiency"? Will a hundred thousand after taxes even do? If so, why do those who have it strive the harder for more?

Any user of the phrase "economic sufficiency" is invited to state its meaning in dollars and cents at any moment and in relation to the buying power of the dollar at that moment. At what point does sufficiency cause added demand to die away, status quo in fiscal circumstances to level off?

The same question is equally valid in the USSR. And it is one that Mao couldn't answer and hasn't even contemplated.

The matter becomes either a joke or insane, depending on one's reality sense, when it is seen that virtually all the student activist leaders railing against American materialism are the sons and daughters of the more affluent or most affluent parents, products of the best-educated, best-heeled, most liberal, most intellectual parents in the land.

They are young people who take for granted their paid-for affluence, their lifelong access to the cornucopia of goods and services, their large allowances, cars, clothes, expensive educations, everything—and they are literally unable to imagine that situation as other than a "right" or as one that their very goals would deprive them of. All they can imagine is, that this "right" ought to be everybody's. That it is not, outrages them.

A system on which all people, from birth to their ages of eighteen, twenty-five—and even up to thirty, cannot float in effortless luxury, is, to them, obviously intolerable. The people who cannot drift down easy river on similar, gilded air mattresses have, clearly, been gypped.

Moreover, certain by-products of the system that keeps the river flowing and the mattresses inflated offend them. These by-products are the biospheric pollutants that have recently been made the new enemy of the rebels. They are evangelical anti-pollutionists. But they are still against irrelevant studies, science and technology above all. So they don't have any real intention to learn what pollution is or how to stop it— for loud yelling of mobs merely shifts local smog and ground pollution.

Yet these are among the people who, by A.D. 2000, will assume to be "in charge" of the establishment and system, always granting civilization persists to that near date.

Who else could buy a new car—to bury!—as a symbol of anything save affluence and asininity? Who but these fools *would* if they were able? Soviets? Or would a new-car funeral be all that big with Mao?

6. The Transmogrification of Mom

More than a quarter of a century ago a well-understood condition of motherhood was named "momism" by this observer. The effect was electrifying. To this day I receive letters and newspaper clippings referring to my "lies about motherhood" and to my "hatred of women."

Actually, momism concerned two special kinds of "moms," described long before as "destroying mothers" and "seductive mothers," who are equally destroying, but in another way. They are psychological "types" and were well known to psychologists. But the fact that I put their jargon into words any layman could understand, and so exposed a wretched truth about millions of mothers to a wide readership, served a purpose. After my somewhat ribald exposition of "momism" a great many psychologists got up the nerve to produce books on the same subject, using my brashness as their icebreaker.

There was a more general meaning in "momism" than the pathological too. Many mothers who were not actually "moms" were infected with mom-like attitudes. America was being poisoned by the growing idea that motherhood, per se, was "sacred." Too many mothers were trying to take the place of fathers, partly owing to pop's cop-out of his duty as a man and male parent, allegedly because of the pressures of business or the job, partly because mother had convinced him that she knew what a man should be and represent better than he did, and partly because of divorces that gave her sole or major custody of the kids.

Women, I pointed out, were doing the majority of the family buying, many held the purse strings and they were beneficiaries of pop's alimony, of his insurance and estate since he died first. So women had much to say about what was manufactured, about what services were required, about the substance of education (as in the PTA), about taste and manners (or the lack of both), and women were the ones who bore down on men to get with it, make more dough to provide more "advantages" for the family—said advantages being, of course, largely mother-defined.

"Mom," I wrote, "is the American Pope. . . . In the hierarchy of miscellaneous articles she is next to the Bible and the Flag." She was trying, I said, to get on top of both. "Mom," I explained, "is a jerk."

Another somber truism was noted: that tendering the vote to females had not in any discernible way provided the "moral uplift" to our culture that had been promised. Ever since woman's suffrage the moral state of the nation has steadily deteriorated, or so people say.

And, of course, as I also made clear, no woman on earth can ever represent or symbolize a male for her sons and daughters. But by psychologically courting her sons in that perverse delusion she emasculates all and makes many into homosexuals. Her daughters will then court pop, or pop-symbols, in emulation. On the other hand, the mom who sees "manhood" as authoritarian and tries to act out the male's role by tyrannizing over her sons and daughters, belittling her spouse and demeaning males in general, will make worms of her boys and sharks of her daughters. Both sorts of mothers will thereby rear addled and rebellious young.

Momism was and is common enough though I would assume, from the masses of evidence published by the experts after my brazen thrust gave them the gall, actual "moms," the conspicuous seducers and destroyers, gooey or Hitlerian, amounted and may still amount only to about one American mother in ten.

Woman's "influence" on the culture, however, was and remains both potent and in its net, retarding. The mere fact that females are presumed by the masses to be less rational, less judicious, less reasonable, less logical, more trivial, more attached to material and lesser values, pettier, without much capacity for consistency, concentration or even thought, has, unquestionably, created an environment in which it has been difficult for females to prove anything contrary or even to behave in any different way. They are expected to exhibit a sort of adorable vacuity and when they display other qualities in their marriage-marketable years, it is seen as unsuitable. Such idle facts as that girls in general do better in math in the first eight to twelve years of school, are not entered into the usual, above-sketched image of the right sort of female to court and wed.

So in a broad sense this dire and negative papacy still rules. If the gross national product be considered from the viewpoint of which portion is fabricated for mom (and her kids) and which for pop, it will be seen that, by ruling out military equipment, some hardware, along with some clothing and a part of sporting goods, there is little in the far greater residue that is not turned out for mom and the children, for the home, its contents, its surroundings, our vehicles, the luxuries of vacations, travel and all else.

Those hyperhucksters, radio and TV, along with other

sales media, address themselves to mom and the kids and only seldom, in meager ratio, directly and exclusively to dad. They never solicit mature persons of either sex.

While we do not think of our mighty, technological society as mom-kids oriented to the degree this suggests, it would be useful to try to. For even male garments are mom-purchased to some humiliating degree.

Our agriculture is mechanized. But food-raising is tailored to what mom and her kids want or have been willingly seduced to want. The great combines that sweep the prairies sweep for them and the most masculine cowhand on the farthest-west ranch is raising cattle that will be of a breed that fats up to the specifications of mother and the children. The supermarket is her kingdom, though mom may wheedle pop into pushing the cart. So is every department store and so are most other stores. The great steel mills pour out their lava for the family, and every downtown skyscraper is erected so fathers can work to supply "advantages" demanded by the wife and kiddies. Bridges of steel span great rivers to allow dad to get to the office faster and expedite mother's shopping, her trip to her job, the family junket or the trucking of her goods.

Pesticides are dusted by planes to increase the current bean crop, and the beans are a variety bred to fit the tin cans mom likes. Fishing fleets on foggy banks are fishing for mother's freezer, and the chemical industry extrudes plastics to wrap her purchases of goods and of edibles made more abundant by eutrophic phosphates.

Heavy industry greatly devotes itself to lightening domestic and home-related chores. And, of course, that is what light industry and the service industries, now the greatest of all, are *for*. It is our way of life, our pride, however bizarre the fact of so much technology serving such trifling ends may be.

The American system is in some large part based on style,

even on "built-in obsolescence," and many term it an "economy of waste."

Fashion and built-in obsolescence today characterize artifacts that were formerly and correctly called "durable goods." Any middle-aged father of a middle-class status (and so, now, any average member of the "affluent" population), given the courage, can recall the numbers of automatic refrigerators, dishwashers, clothes washing machines, vacuum cleaners and other such domestic "aids" he paid for. The inventory will likely be a shock owing to the wearing out of these gadgets, or even to the trade-in of still usable items for more stylish types with, often, only trivial "improvements," if any. The dollars down those drains are also the wasted days in his years.

Style as the cause of new purchase is, I think, the result of pressures brought by a wife, a mother or by mom-oriented kids on a male who may not realize what caused that wastage of resources and his life.

He will accept the reason given by his womanfolk and kids: it is his *duty* to keep the place from looking like an old-fashioned junk heap. That "duty" he will have been reared to accept without question and implement to his utmost ability. He may even feel a mother-imbued pride equal to his wife's in this waste that wastes *him*.

Nowadays there's no end to examples of the exploitation of style and fad by industry. And each one testifies to dad's conditioning as a sucker. They exist on every scale. A walk along Park Avenue in New York City, north, from the Grand Central area, will disclose the almost incredible fact that even skyscrapers are erected in changing styles so that one regarded as modern ten or twenty years ago is now plainly antique and those under construction are designed to make the current sort, the "glass boxes," look as démodé as automobiles with fins.

It has been easy in all historic times to change the styles of female dress. Until very recently, though, tailors were anguished by the reluctance of males to depart any great distance from the habit that had been standard since the industrial revolution. Madison Avenue's recent "gray flannel suit" was only an adaptation of what an Englishman had worn in "the City" for generations. Lately, especially in sports and informal and nonbusiness attire, even men have yielded. And the best-dressed business gentlemen in Manhattan have gone so far lately as to come to their offices in colored and patterned shirts. Some even wear loafers.

But the changes in male clothing styles have been urged on them by females. And it took a century of such urging to dent the long custom of the business uniform.

It is important to get this clear perspective on style and on the resulting waste among American adults before taking the next and more cogent step.

American youth is indoctrinated from infancy in this same, synthetic concept of status shown by style, novelty, change and turnover. From very early in life, *toys* teach both girls and boys that short-lived possessions and rapid changes are prestige gauges. How many annual billions are spent on children's toys, clothes, sports goods and accessories is, again, a figure probably obtainable by an economist with steady nerves and one I would rather not know.

Childhood is now largely a training period for consumers. Style and built-in obsolescence are encountered in the kindergarten if not the cradle. Toys are not constructed to last but to come apart quickly. Children are TV taught to feel shame at the idea of durability in playthings. What's old but usable is dated. It lacks appurtenances found on the latest models. What boy is coasting, still, on grandpa's sled? What girl is using mother's dolls? The sled has no motor and the dolls cannot pee.

Little girls bake cookies in electric ovens that do the job with a light bulb. And boys are briefed by stages for the blissful day when they are granted a permit to drive real cars. They will by then have flown planes with miniature gas engines, operated mini-cycles and gone on to mini-cars.

Commerce has abetted this infernal process with self-serving brilliance. The period of youth is now broken into arbitrary categories. Once, there were just children who became minors before they were adult. Now, American kids are toddlers, pre-schoolers, pre-teens and teen-agers. Small wonder that, at twenty-one, their exploited lives lead them to invent one more kind of people, people under thirty. This is to be expected in a nation with such absurd ground rules. Recent studies have shown that one fundamental trouble with under-thirty rebels is owing to our national extension of adolescence beyond the point at which less commercial societies demand a high degree of independence and self-sufficiency.

People over eighteen, or twenty-one, at least, have invented a next stage, lasting twelve or at least nine years, not because they are different, or brighter and more virtuous than the over-thirties, but because they yearn to remain in the only state they knew, a category of immaturity.

Their massive indictment of their elders is then but camouflage for an inculcated infantilism.

Each consumer-making false stage connotes a next and even more gratifying category. So, perhaps, when a larger number of the under-thirty rebels go over that Niagara, they will invent yet another category to occupy as juveniles.

The stages produce other effects. Each has its special costumes, rituals and toys, too. Pre-schooler, pre-teen, teen-ager and so on have rigid rules for goods consumption. The day a boy or girl makes a shift, everything he or she owns, wears and enjoys changes, too. There are styles for these sham intervals and woe betide the parents who send Willie or Maybelle off to class or turn them out to play—with "outgrown" garments or equipment.

Even people on welfare try to furnish their children with this mode-fast bounty. Affluent parents not only use such goods to avoid the bore of rearing their young, but their media-trained, TV-brainwashed offspring neither expect nor want love and care. They want the age-group "necessities" shown on the tube. So nobody is much or at all aware of our trade of junk for love.

Perhaps this slick system for rearing kids as consumers explains more about young Americans than has been noted. It is this group that has the greatest proportion of the most lethal automobile accidents, for instance. Yet they are supposed to be relatively brighter than we were and they definitely have, on the average, better vision, better hearing and faster reflexes. Nobody has demonstrated that their death-wish is outsize. Rather, the opposite seems the case if one notes that their reluctance to be drafted for war is based on the statistically-thin argument that they don't want to be killed.

But these are the highest-rated of the car-killed. Can it be owing to their toy-hood? Are cars just toys to teen-agers and to people under thirty?

When one realizes what tremendous effort has gone into making toys "fool proof" and notes how many risky toys of yore are taboo (fireworks, to name one sort), the foregoing idea becomes persuasive. A car is something to have fun with—till it kills you, or your passenger, or till you get the idea a car isn't a plaything, by lucky maturation.

Perhaps, too, that unconscious toy sense explains many other manifestations of the young, their vandalism or their eagerness to burn down the Science Building—as, they say, the only means for getting attention. Maybe, to a consumer-trained generation no thing is more than a toy. Their prior experience of life taught that every artifact is disposable and even a skyscraper is subject to rapid obsolescence owing to changing styles. Nothing real is even meant to have permanency, in their view.

That may also be the reason for their widespread regard of history as "irrelevant." A glance into history suggests that man's past and what man raised up in it were durable. Chartres cannot be tossed out like Chux.

Again, if durability is seen as liability, the years beyond thirty may suggest that odious aspect. The kids who have been reared to value not what is theirs but what will be theirs at the next shift to the pre-teens or the teens now face a life in which there is no further hope of new categories with new toys and clothes and customs. It may seem not only unfamiliar but unbearable. In any event, they have done their best to dispose of all people "over thirty."

In a similar way, young radicals may see the plight of people who never managed to attain the standard American cornucopia-sequence—the poor, the black—as intolerable. Greed is their religion and it is projected on the have-nots as if in righteousness. The one important permanence they know is steady turnover. And, of course, people nowadays in some unprecedented numbers can "afford" this eternal parade of purchase. The very reason they can afford it is that their indulgence in the affair makes them affluent. What keeps the GNP growing enables them to squander it.

The fault, and that word is mild for what is ecologically suicidal, is not solely American or exclusively a fault of free nations. Red greed is identical though not yet as effectively fomented by media or as overfurnished with supplies. The Red world, like the disadvantaged world, is racing to catch up. For all "economies," like our own, do and increasingly will depend on an everlasting escalation of production and distribution.

It is the firm belief of nearly every sociologist, economist, political scientist, liberal and intellectual, so, in effect, of nearly all *people*, that more money, for the purpose of providing more food, more goods, medical care, more factories, roads, machines, of building bigger schools and of extending the educational years to some indefinite number, will "solve" our problems, including those of poverty, crime, violence, of the rejected blacks and everything else, the above note on present realities of our "standard" is important.

Americans, about a sixteenth of the world's people, now consume from a third to a half of all the raw materials taken from the planet's mines, oil wells, quarries, from its farms and croplands, from its forests and other sources. Much of it is finally scattered into the air or seas, rusts into the earth or is reduced one or more stages toward entropy by the uses we make of it. We do not even return the fertility of what we eat to the production of more food. We are, then, losing, beyond recovery, or to a degree where recovery does not "pay," a hogged share of the world's resources.

But the rebellious young Americans demand billions for the aid of people lacking their "advantages" and at the same time assert that the system, the establishment and lifeways of their parents (who built the first and are the second) cannot be borne *because they are so materialistic.*

However "idealistic" they deem such intentions, they ought to see where the limits arise—and those limits may be reached within a decade, even for this one nation.

They should also see that if the social and political "evils" they decry, and often with reason, are to be ameliorated even in USA, what must first be completely changed is their own attitude toward "living standards." For America's present affluence," let alone its planned goods increase and its wider distribution, cannot long proceed on any scale now imagined. Not only is it inconceivable that a sixteenth of living peoples will long be able to monopolize from a third to a half of everything the world produces, but the USA cannot long continue to produce what it consumes at home, per capita. The environment will not allow the procedure endlessly.

But to alter even the production means that damage the environment at a cumulative rate would mean that the cost of *every* item in the GNP would be so increased that the current living standard would be priced out of existence. We cannot long keep what we have. We cannot long augment that. And we neither can nor will be able to make more for have-not hordes.

America, with all other technically "advanced" nations and with those that are merely becoming technological, will very soon be forced to make immense and shattering revisions of industry, of uses of raw materials and means and rates of distribution of commodities and services it supplies. The most rational step toward that would be to return to standards of durability. If, for just one instance, a car can be made to last thirty years, every new car owner should then be able to buy only a thirty-year-car and obliged to keep it that long. But even that minor, truly trivial revision would, of course, destroy our economy; and it would equally reverse Communist goals.

Though adaptation to reality is essential, the effort cannot be undertaken, even at some perhaps economically feasible rate, until and unless there is a beginning of an understanding of the irrationalism of our technological faith. People, whatever their age, who resent the "materialism" of our present style of life yet wish to extend its boons to posterity and to those not now beneficiaries, may believe they are bright, but if they are they will need to prove it by, say, walking on water.

To cite women, even the moms, as particularly responsible for America's economy of display, style, waste and planned obsolescence is fair in one way. In another, it is not. Male Americans weren't forced by law or torture to enter into this business of affluence-through-sabotage. Nobody had to create markets for nothing-products, or for disposable and self-destroying goods. Nobody had to raise American living standards—so-called—to our fantastic level, that idiot peak at which one finds in supermarkets nonfoods on sale for people who have already eaten too much but wish to go on eating!

This "no-calorie," "diet food," "non-fattening" business symbolizes our present way of life quite well. It also characterizes our economy. It is the proof of our greed. Millions starve and billions soon may but America goes on eating nothing-meals though grossly overweight.

A common analogue for current "moral" behavior is "ancient Rome." It is not fitting as employed. The "moral decline" in Rome that is widely held to be the sign of Rome's imminent fall and so, predictive of our own, refers to sex "morals." That use is as idiotic as most of the tawdry "parallels" Americans pervert to support their bigotries. Sex "morals" have nothing to do with other "moralities" and Rome did not collapse because of fornication or promiscuity—these had marked the entire Roman epoch and were general among so-called pagans up to the time the Christians made men lesser than pagans.

Where America resembles old Rome is in the non-sexual ways noted here, those of waste, affluence and gross materialism, in, then, the education for greed. The old Romans didn't know anything about calories and nothing about how to extract nourishment from food so that non-food could be devoured, stuff that felt fat in the mouth and tasted sweet. They had no technology for bottling nothing-cola. The decadent Romans simply ate their fill and went out to vomit so they could gorge themselves again. That is what the consumers of no-calorie and "diet" foods and drinks do, here.

That is the philosophy of our economy.

The man who trades in a car because it is out of style, or because it has deteriorated in a few years to a tacky state, is, simply, a man who consumes grossly and then disgorges to consume anew. Industry, through advertising, makes that both necessary and automatic—by keeping its finger in the American gullet, diddling incessantly.

On first notice of this fact it may seem inexplicable that the sons and daughters of the affluent, intellectual, liberal, educated, top stratum of our society constitute the activists and mutineers on campus, the opponents of what they learned and are.

It takes more acuity than the involved students have to see how this contradiction came about. It starts with their sense of adult sickness and their note of its materialist cause. They can see the older generation is ecologically wanton. But what they fail to perceive in their merely responsive nausea is that they, too, are vomiting because the same finger constantly pokes at their gag reflex. They but demand their own "too much" for all who have too little.

That sets up a wild and mind-blown scene.

The spinning mills and garment factories are roaring to make their costumes. A huge industry thunders to keep them supplied with this year's dress: the beads, the brief shape of them, the moment's fashion in pants, the sandals from dead cattle, the current configuration and size of sunglasses, the overcoats of momentarily proper length and cut. Next year the corporation will retool to sell the post-mod array. Junior walks hand in hand with his chick to the beauty parlor where he, too, will get the coiffure this month demands.

He has his car: now, a small sports model; tomorrow, some other sort. He is as much a vomiter-to-eat-anew as his mom and pop. And while he can see how wretched the values of his parents are, how dismal life is for them, and the fact that their depersonalized and avaricious state has something to do with their materialism, he never stops to note that his righteous anger, his perception of the cause of what he detests in them, is, also, *his* way of life.

And then he says it isn't fair that others lack what he has!

But when does any young American even whisper the basic truth of everybody's common lunacy, here?

On what campus has what young rebel ever set down notes of what he will *do without*, as a means, the *only* means, to diminish the economy of vomit?

A few hippie-types have gone back to "nature" in communities in the woods. But they are not campus rebels, activists, SDS yahoos, antipollution zealots. And they have not proven their experiments in minimal possessing will endure. Their children, like the children of Village East, will still require the sophisticated services of medicine and public health just to survive in a nationally acceptable way. And they, too, as parents, will still be parasitical in a degree only slightly lesser than the total parasitism of other technological men. Even such very tentative and probably soon-to-be-abandoned attempts to escape the system will not attract enough people to slow a single production line. And the environs of these communes will continue to be contaminated, exhausted and downgraded so the members will not escape what they imagine they have escaped.

The people under thirty will show that their claim to relatively more knowledge than any prior generation is at least beginning to be valid when their acts reveal that they really do know what is wrong with adults and elders . . . and that it is exactly what is wrong with themselves.

It isn't surprising, then, that these youths often attempt to call attention to their and the nation's dismal condition by destroying property. Such acts truly reveal their ingrained conviction, the one I've implied, that nothing made by men is important because if it comes apart it will be replaced, and with something "better," that is, more modish if equally perishable.

The generations that built durable goods and into them built as much durability as possible had a million times as much actual knowledge as these young oafs.

For, since the resources of the planet are finite, thrift, not waste, is wise . . . unless the meaning of man-now is all the meaning man plans to have.

Such reality, however, is not one the young know or plan to study.

From that true viewpoint they are all, all the LIE people, not merely ignorant but *functionally illiterate.*

7. The Sons, the Daughters, the Logical Heritage

It is easy for an adult American to say that the young mutineers, as they seize campus buildings, hold deans and professors hostage, ravage files and generally behave like every mob on the rampage, are "spoiled rotten."

It is a term my peer group often uses.

That it may be fitting will have no effect on the offenders. *Something* ails them.

Their claim against adult society is an unending list of such horrors and boredoms, frivolities, political and military follies and viciousnesses, moral failures, and such massive evidence of dishonesty, self-deceit and general hypocrisy, that, were it valid, not merely some young people but all sane persons of all ages would or should rebel and with whatever rational means needed to bring change.

The criticisms are valid.

That, I can say with a certain composure. For, as an author, I began to put forth in books and various other media, precisely the same damning claims against my fellow citizens as the young rebels are making.

My first published book, a novel that appeared more than

forty years ago, was just such an assault on our sexual
hypocrisy, our cheesy values, our spreading dishonesty, and
our national failure to face truth or accept reality. That
other book in which a chapter was devoted to "mom's" presumed tastes, *Generation of Vipers,* appeared more than a
quarter of a century ago and contained a detailed, chapter-
by-chapter indictment of educators and education, common
man, military men, doctors, economists, the liberal-intellectual establishment, the scientific establishment, businessmen
and various other types and groups.

Nine-tenths of the enraged criticisms voiced by indignant
youth comes to me, therefore, with a repetitive sound, that
of the ribald and furious outrage I expressed in the very
same terms, and often, harsher ones, before the vast majority
of people under thirty were even born.

Until the past five or six years, in consequence, I have
stood well up in the opinion of whatever portion of young
persons of high school and more especially college age found
the folkways of the USA contemptible and fraudulent. But it
has been difficult at times and often impossible for me to
understand certain of the responses of the recent angry
generation to those same (and now almost innate as well
as more widely spread) evils and idiocies of my era and theirs.

A little more than a year ago, however, my daughter,
her husband and my wife finally, and after so acrimonious
an argument I feared I might have lost the affection of all
three, managed to show me where at least part of my dis-
sympathy was, itself, erroneous.

It does no good, I must first explain, so the question will
not be held in suspense, to ask anybody of my age, or
even of age fifty or forty, what he or she "would do" were
he or she now eighteen, or twenty, or twenty-five.

Nobody can answer that question.

To look back on a life of conspicuous rebellion, as to

dress, thinking, attitude and other matters in my high school years, looking at myself as a college dropout who departed in anger at least as heated as any now to be seen, gives me no answer. I was a public and violent critic of the establishment, system, values and manners in USA, of our general beliefs, pretenses and the rest, but even so, I have no notion of where I would stand, today, as a college student.

If, with so early, parallel and unusual a record, I cannot imagine my reactions in the present were I under thirty, nobody can. To say or think otherwise is, simply, to say one knows very little of one's self. It is to state one knows little of one's self at earlier ages, also.

It is an exercise in vanity.

However, the enlightenment which follows was not gained by retrospect but owing to the vehemence, perseverence, articulateness and temper of my family. My conversion occurred in the nick of time . . . only days before it was to serve me in a crisis.

The "crisis" occurred recently and I was brought into it by my wife. "While you were out," she said, "a young man phoned. He is president of the Student Union at the University. He wants you to come over next Wednesday and have a dialogue with whatever students or faculty people care to attend the meeting. They have a big hall for you and expect a good crowd." She expected me to go, I saw.

The name of the university is not important; it was a state university and a large one; naming it would merely reduce the general worth of what follows and it has wide applicability. I returned the call of the student government president. He suggested that, if I would appear, I should speak for ten minutes and then throw open the meeting to the so-called "dialogue." I agreed.

Local papers carried an announcement the next day and my presence was due the day after. I was glad my family had just "converted" me. Otherwise, I would have aroused an unguessable amount of hostility in whatever student audience I might have, in an agreed hour of dialogue. These were, at the moment, in "riot." There had been anger and dissension for a year owing to the firing of a professor for unjust administrative "reasons." Recently, two student-admired instructors had been refused tenure after they had announced their decision to concentrate on teaching and abandon work toward doctoral degrees. That snub of the sacred Ph.D. had so angered the management that this pair had been chopped off, too.

The result was the now-familiar one. Swarms of wrathful students had seized and were occupying main buildings. The campus was in tumult. Other buildings were being menaced. Meetings were occurring everywhere. Classes were becoming impossible to hold. In sum, my appearance would coincide with the peaking of a potentially dangerous situation.

One of my well-heeled friends invited me to lunch on the day the papers printed the notice of that impending dialogue. I had no other date and no idea of his urgency until we sat down together for lunch. He was so worried about my safety, when he found me determined to show up in the maelstrom, that he tried to insist on hiring twenty-five private detectives, dressed to look like students or instructors, who would take front rows and be prepared to protect me from injury—armed with weapons of sorts scaled for whatever degree of threat I would find myself facing. It took most of the luncheon hour to convince him I wanted no part of such a squad and that I meant what I kept saying:

"If I can't talk to and with a bunch of college students without being clobbered I feel I must give up writing, as unfit for it in present times."

A sturdy boast which I hoped would hold true, at least insofar as being clobbered was concerned, but one which my

friend's anxiety and his repeated offer did little to re-enforce.
In any case, I showed up at the student government president's rooms and was driven to what proved to be a large
and crowded hall. Later, another friend, an exceedingly
astute scientist, told me I had acted "unfairly" and it was
a moment before I realized that crack was one of his typical
ironies. . . .

After a swift introduction by the young president I spoke
for much less than ten minutes.

What I said was what I had just learned from my family
at such passing emotional cost to all four of us.

I agreed that the administration, in canning a professor,
and now, two popular instructors, had behaved abominably,
violating freedom and the very meaning of teaching, not to
mention human and constitutional rights, as well as due
process. I said that; and I said I knew how they felt and
what had driven them to riotous acts then escalating; and I
said their sentiments were, basically, very "American."

"You tried all legal avenues of approach and all possible
means of obtaining redress, short of violence, you could think
of. They flopped. So, you took the present step, one you see
as analogous to the Boston Tea Party." They looked interested. "When a Boston Tea Party fails to call attention to intolerable injustice, you feel, as those others did in colonial
America, that nothing remains but Lexington and Concord."

Here, I need to note a handicap of all verbal people.
We cannot seem to understand what we have no word
for.

It was my recollection of the first steps in our Revolution
that led me, that night of the family debate, to understand
what my wife, daughter and son-in-law were trying to explain
about young rebels. When I thought of the Tea Party I was
suddenly able to comprehend the feelings of young mutineers,

or, at least, of those whose motives were just and moods, justly furious.

At that time, I'd not heard anybody use the Tea Party analogue for young violence. But since I did so, it has appeared frequently in the endless discussions of rebellious youth. Things get around. Nevertheless, the usual reference to Boston's tea-dumping is now used, by critics of the young, to say there is *no* analogue or comparison in the two sorts of mutinies. What those pseudo-precisionists fail to observe is that young people *feel* the way the taxed but unrepresented colonials felt. The analogue is for the feeling, not for ensuing acts.

Of course, no sensible person will imagine that the violent deeds of young activists are as justified as those of the Boston protesters who jettisoned tea. But if people, young or old, believe themselves as unfairly trapped, as atrociously penalized, as greatly victimized by injustice, the nature of their response is not the question but only a sign of the intensity of their ire, which can reach the Tea Party level. The most justifiable rage does not excuse mania. The victimized Bostonians, for example, did not present "non-negotiable" demands. They simply went to war when their honorable demands were ignored. That is different, an act with a goal, not merely a feeling of frustration transmuted into pointless vandalism.

Here at this university the image, the semantic I'd found for my own understanding, fitted well, up to a point. The students had borne three sets of injustices, vicariously, in part, but personally, in their deprivation of three good faculty members. They had tried, for more than a year in the first case, all legal means for just response. Those failed and, instead, the same administrative affront had recurred, twice, in this term.

So they were, for a fact, Boston Tea Party mad. And they took steps somewhat similar, though far less destructive, here, as will be shown. Adult pompoids, columnists, statesmen, commentators and all such had better get straightened out on this matter of student anger. For wherever it rises from such a cause as launched the Boston sabotage, even though that cause be lesser in degree, the *wrath* is a real emotion of young people who want justice, and have been robbed of it.

It is only when young fury rises from concepts that are irrational, untrue, senseless, ignorant, politically and socially stupid or corrupt and without any aim but havoc, that adults have any right to deplore their *rage*. What they then *do,* whether their ire is based in reality or whether it is not, must be seen as something else. An adult who cannot understand those differences—as I couldn't till that time—certainly will be unable to communicate with youth and youth with him.

That much understanding is mandatory. Without it, an adult is merely self-righteous and a fool, too, which, of course, means I was long self-righteous and a great fool about the mutinies of students, insofar as understanding their causal feelings was concerned. I don't *mind* having been ignorant, stupid, a fool, unjust and full of other faults. I still am. What I do mind is maintaining that poor condition of my brain when a way is presented which would alleviate it, and I then fail to take that path. That, too, can happen.

Such rigidity is near to universal, however, and all any human being can do is to notice and diminish the state as much as he is able. Most, don't even try, don't even know they are poker-stiff in mind and heart. That, indeed, is what youth most detests, and rightly detests, in others—and often fails to see in itself.

During the dialogue or "confrontation" I am about to describe, a wonderful example of what is meant, here, cropped up. Throughout the exposure, I smoked cigarettes.

At one point a student put up her hand and asked, "If you value man so much, and reason, logic, truth, besides, how do you explain the fact that you are almost a chain-smoker?"

I answered at once with what was an evident truth: "It is an act of utter and total hypocrisy."

That produced one of the biggest hands I was ever given—long and thunderous applause, stamping and whistles.

Its vehemence astonished me until, later, I realized my trivial confession represented, probably, the first time many of those students had ever heard a grown person, in public, instantly, honestly and unaffectedly admit what is true in many ways of us all: "I am a hypocrite."

It was what *they* had been incessantly saying of *us*. The novelty of hearing it from an adult was the cause for their astonishing approval. And that, in turn, is a good gauge, reader, if you are an adult, of how giant, remorseless and stony a damned hypocrite *you* and most adults are!

But to return to the main scene . . .

My Tea Party allusion and opener gained me considerable respect and time enough to add the only other item I had planned:

"My one question about your rebellion has nothing to do with your mood or the means you've chosen to emphasize that. You wish, or many of you do, to smash the establishment and system. We are agreed it merits little support, as is. But assume that you succeed. Assume your righteousness, and it *is* often rightful, leads to the demolition of the target. At that point, then, you, yourselves, having won, will *be* the establishment and system. What plans have you for that event?"

They talked and I did. The hour passed. Some students left for classes or to relieve building-occupiers. Some faculty members had to depart, others appeared. A second hour went by. Then, after a *third* hour of that dialogue I was obliged from sheer exhaustion to make my apologies and scram. . . .

My ironic friend didn't mean it was a dirty trick to open the dialogue as I have said. He meant it was astute to begin with that central question before the audience could question *me*.

Of course, they did that . . . for a bit more than three hours.

But I had obliged them to put their queries in the frame of reference I'd established.

What would they do if they won?

It was not a matter that had occurred to many of them, plainly.

Victory was so remote that any thought of it, let alone, of times beyond, was not—call it, "revelant." Yet they could see the point. As the talk continued they could also see that I understood their indignations and had felt them, and written about them, for those forty years.

I am happy to be able to report that, on this occasion in this university, the president resigned, the professor and two instructors were restored to the faculty and when the building-occupiers left, they cleaned up the premises so no trace of their illegal presence remained. That, I know, is not regulation for such a rumble, but it was true in this case.

Not, of course, that I had anything to do with it—the decent release of buildings when the terms were met or the subsequent, peaceful resumption of classes.

But my question remains.

And no answers are coming in.

The New Left has no answers.

What argument is advanced by these liberal, intellectual idealists, as they assume they are, is, simply, that they find it not necessary to know how to right a wrong simply because they've pointed it out as such.

That, of course, is true.

The critic is not required to find the means to mend, change, improve or erase what he has shown faulty. His function is complete when he has made a valid criticism. And no improvement of any sort can be made in a person, product, establishment, system or theory unless someone *has* faulted it. Until then, it will be, by definition, presumed all right or even perfect. However, after the critic has functioned, somebody, not he necessarily, but *somebody*, will have to find means to remove, improve, or repair the fault, or else, again by definition, the critic will have spoken in vain.

That situation is one I understand as a man who has made and published thousands of criticisms which, I believe, were largely valid, and many of which have been proven so by subsequent event and history, but of which very few if any have led to much improvement. That failure in a career as a critic has, in fact, led me to such different efforts as this one, efforts which are intended to present some constructive suggestions.

When, however, I look at the efforts and means the young have widely employed to express anything other than criticisms of the American style and standards, hypocrisies and sins, I find them largely vain.

Cop-out, of course, in ineffective. The critic who makes his statement and then walks away is a coward. He should stand firm and keep talking. Blowing a building or a mind is no help.

The drug scene will be discussed in another chapter but, here, it is sufficient to say that a dependence on chemicals of a known harmful or even of an unknown effect, as a way of

escape from a hateful present, is, again, cop-out. It advances
the drug-taker no inch even as protest and it may endanger
his health and that of his posterity or even cost his life.

Mutiny, the common campus rioting in the varied forms
seen recently, has attracted attention and has caused some
revision of administrative and other policy of loathsome
sorts. It is a procedure of short-term use, however, as the signs
of inevitable "backlash" are already apparent and could and
will (if mutiny is continued) result in repressions of such extreme sorts as to void any gains made by violence.

Mysticism, plunges into the occult, Zen, and the like have
been tried by billions of people in hundreds upon hundreds
of forms, for thousands of years without a sign of any gain.
The recent, now-extensive and still-growing conversion of
American hordes to astrological belief is only one more reason
for all younger people and, indeed, all people of whatever
age, to perceive the minuteness of their knowledge and their
immense capacity for being duped. Under-thirty people who
have engaged in or are engaged in tendering the slightest
credulity to astrology have lost their franchise to carp at older
people about anything whatever.

Zen and allied occultist enterprises fall in almost as preposterous a category.

Having often stated elsewhere that I am a Jung-affirmed
authority on Jungian theory, I have implied—to all persons
cognizant of Jung's work—a considerable insight into the
"wisdom" or "philosophy" of the East.

It was Jung's mastery of that area of perception and reflection which led him to realize that Freud's theories were
related to the European culture only, and not, therefore,
of sufficient breadth. Oriental or Eastern insights also enabled Jung to add the great concept of "collective unconscious" to psychological hypothesis and to elucidate, in terms
understandable in the West, the "law of opposites" or "yang-

yin" principle, along with the meaning of their "transcendence," a third major contribution.

But a young person who leaps into the arcane exercises of as special and abstruse a sort as those of Zen, without any wider knowledge of psychology or of philosophy, will find the discipline only slightly and briefly rewarding, or so-seeming, if that. It is intended as a means toward gaining *individual,* not "social," insights and even those gurus who practice the obscure and arduous rites usually find they have been rewarded, if at all, only after a decade or two of effort—and effort that will have been their single enterprise, all that while. This is not a business for casual kids.

Implicit in the youthful revolt against older people and their standards and practices is, of course, a revolt against Christianity, or, at least, what is called and claimed to be one or another sort of that. I assume, since nothing else is assumable, that the New Left is at least as atheistic as was the Old, and probably more so, owing to the availability of clearer data substantiating the atheistic or at least the agnostic position. God is not dead; he never was.

If young people have not asked believers to describe a "God" in whom the inquirers can then discover a scintilla of sensible or even imaginable evidence on which to base agreement, they should do so at once. For the more truth one learns, the more real and broad one's education becomes, the more obvious it grows that all man's images of "God" are exactly that, fantasies, beyond any possible definition, and fantasies, moreover, invented for vain causes that are now abundantly manifest and manifest as self-deceits. The Christian pantheon is as variable and multiple as the Hindu.

Except for worthless examples of mysticism, cop-out, mind-blowing and of superstition, young rebellious Americans give little evidence of any expectation of finding or even of seeking means for managing the world they aim to shatter and, if they do it, will have to control or try to. But they have avoided the equally untenable cop-out by "faith."

Certainly, neither Zen nor astrology nor any occult, abstruse, mythical or nakedly superstitious ideology offers means to manage a technological society that will have been deprived of its current system and suffered a deposing of management. The reign of God is over, too.

I have already argued that the Marxist "analysis" is blunder-riddled even though the New Left clings to it still. I have further shown that the New Left cannot possibly propose a Marxist "synthesis" owing in part to the many and uniformly horrible examples of that job, visible today.

The complete rejection of our society, undertaken by the Haight-Asbury hippies, was, of course, equally fallacious from its inception. Somebody has to produce food and clothing and shelter, bear and rear children and so forth. Those latter-day hippies and their kindred souls now making a Rousseau-like effort to live simply in small, rural, self-supporting communes are, as I've said, too, self-deluded.

As a youth trained for that venerable and ideal operation of entering the north woods in the spring, naked, with nothing but an ax, and coming out in the autumn ready for winter and so for indefinite survival—and as a World War II expert on sea-survival—I can state unequivocally that even the minimal requirement is of an ax, in the woods, and of fishing gear, at sea; and neither furnishes a happy way of existence, let alone a way to bring up children decently.

My assault on our technological society, my long one, often leads to a peculiar response of possible relevance, here— the statement that what I recommend is some sort of wilderness-survival, or tepee-wood-bark-root-soup way of life, for all. I have never said anything of the sort and never remotely suggested that kind of existence as ideal, meaningful, desirable or even a thinkable goal.

I used to wonder how on earth so many thousands of my readers could infer from my criticisms of our condition and culture that I meant we should return to wild living, or to living as the commune folks feign they are doing.

In time, however, that odd reaction became understandable to me. A majority even of those Americans who are able to read books is so committed to and involved with technology as to see *any* suggestion of *any* reduction of goods and services as a threat to everything. Thus, the previous chapter, in which it was pointed out that the American standard of living and the American economy of an ever-bigger GNP cannot long be sustained, implies that a certain fraction of readers will write to me asking again why I think living in a branch lean-to, clad in raw skins and eating roots, is an improvement.

Every such reaction provides a gauge of the blank-minded servitude of Americans to the system as-is, to its means, management and artifacts. Any suggestion that these should be decreased, modified or altered is then seen as meaning a reversion to the naked and miserable lifeways of the now extinct Tierra del Fuegians. Opponents of the system take note. That is the measure of its hold over multitudes! How do you smash *them?*

8. Nobody Listens

As I was rewriting these animadversions I happened to notice on a rack of paperbacks a title that caught my attention because of its mnemonic effect. A good friend of mine, the late author-psychologist Robert Lindner, had written a book entitled *Rebel Without a Cause;* this title was *Rebel Without a Program.*

The author was George F. Kennan, statesman and historian, and I bought and read the volume. It reprinted a lecture Mr. Kennan had delivered and the New York *Times* had later published, a lecture about our angry young. The book also contained a fair number of letters from young Americans and older ones expressing assorted reactions to the lecture-essay. A third section was a reply by Mr. Kennan to those young dissidents, an attempt to straighten them out about what he had said as well as to point out the many examples of non-think and illogic in their heated and rather juvenile responses.

It must be noted that Mr. Kennan put forward many of the arguments I, too, have set down to show the blank, emotional ineptitude of the activist young. I could and per-

haps should add that various other authors, among them
Sidney Hook, have also stated, in their ways, similar criticisms of the mixed bag of kids whose bag is being mixed up.
However, since the first draft of this manuscript was written
before I had deliberately (and, in Mr. Kennan's case, ac-
cidentally) studied the literature of back talk by adults addressed to youth, and since many of the ideas used here
appeared in that first text in one form or another, I feel free
to assert that none of my opinions is borrowed or plagiarized.

I am, however, now aware that various lines of parallel
detestation, revulsion and deserved criticism originated in
minds of other adults than myself. That fact may give parts
of this effort a trite sound, as, indeed, I was aware would be
the case to a degree, since I could hardly suppose that I,
alone, had seen all that ailed a large, largely youthful, very
sick portion of the population.

Others, then, have indicated such truths as that one presented in the previous chapter: the young people who so
ardently wish to alter the values and lifeways of present-day
America are not looking, or even willing to look at those
greatest evils, errors and social sins which it will be their lot
to bear as consequences, knowledge of which is their necessity
for remedy or even for mere human survival.

Mr. Kennan, and no doubt others, have supplied yet
another insight into the mindless mutineers.

They cannot talk much.

Their vocabulary is meager, vague and limited.

All they know—and I think I have added some clarifica-
tion to the cause of that picayune mask of sophistication—
is what they have gathered from the teaching, texts, lectures
and literature of the LIE and especially its social and political
exponents.

Youthful enthusiasm over what youth calls a "participatory
democracy," for example, merely employs a phrase borrowed

from social science that stands for something the young
advocates are, as is already evident, utterly unable to partic-
ipate in, even if they could bring about such a "democracy."

Just as their "New Left" can be shown to be intellectually
sleazy and, to the extent that it is "left" in the older sense,
absurd, so any and every verbal formulation on which these
mini-minds stand so ardently can be exposed as unsound, the
mere head-noises of a quack-vocabulary.

"Confrontation," for another instance, has an evanescent
meaning as a local event designed to attract attention; but
when the question "Attention to what?" is answered by endless
negatives, the term itself becomes void.

One agrees that it is theoretically and actually possible to
call a war "immoral." But unless one means by the word that
all war is immoral, one has assumed the duty of defining
"moral war." Without that definition, the claim of the immorality of a particular conflict can have no meaning. But I
have not heard any youthful definition of moral war, its
nature, condition and limits.

If we are ever to gain awareness of the *hope* toward which
I am patiently making my way, it will be possible only after
we examine and discard those values, concepts, aims, notions,
claims, led cheers and non-ideas that are widespread, that
often are all but universal, but that promise no hope at all and,
instead, guarantee a constant diminution of what hope we
might hold without them.

The most dismally mistaken of all young plaints is their
incessant claim that *nobody listens to them.*

The truth is exactly opposite.

Too Goddamn many people listen to them . . . *too seriously.*

There is a large segment of the adult citizenry of USA
that goes around either with a smug smile or a hushed scare-
tone, saying, *You better listen to the kids. They have something to tell us.*

Either posture, the fatuous or the menacing, means, of course, that young America has something *new* to say.

As an adult listener trying to be equable I have yet to hear any sound, however distant and tiny, of this new word, alarming *or* joyful.

Their adverse cavils at the establishment and system, at middle-class values, at the going lifeway of the land, are never novel . . . to me. Every syllable, or nearly that, is, as I hardly need repeat, old stuff and on my record as of decades ago.

In addition, there is a booming, vaster amount of error and sin in our culture that the "unheard" young jerks never mention, or mention merely in passing as a minor smog on the landscape.

Their language doesn't encourage attention on the part of knowledgeable persons. When, for example, a clot of wide-eyed, would-be reformers presents something called "non-negotiable demands," the informed observer merely becomes aware of their infantilism, providing, of course that person is able to accept the truth of this business, that it isn't a callow effort at humor. Surely, such "demands" can be made only by non-persons, rare here but abundant in the USSR.

It will be necessary to examine other aspects of young mindlessness, too, before any positive suggestions can be made in a definite form.

That necessity was made vividly plain by Mr. Kennan's young correspondents. In letter after letter these arrogant pip-squeaks revealed that it was they who didn't listen . . . and didn't, because they couldn't understand any English prose except their own gasbag argot. They wrote letters which they *thought* refuted the gentleman's calm and rather kindly critique. But the letters showed the young correspondents hadn't gathered what Mr. Kennan said and couldn't and so, had no idea what he or they were talking about, or, rather, of what they were not talking about that they *thought* was a real subject.

I suspect that adults who feel that what youth says "better be heard" because it's *ominous* are, merely, people with a guilty knowledge, a faintly conscious sense of their own mean acts in support of the evils in the system and establishment.

For any such, the imprecation that the kids have something we better hear in akin to a confessional mass. They feel shriven by threatening others out of what is actually their own bad conscience.

The fatuous ones are worse, in my view.

For these appear to believe not only that the young rebels are on target as critics but that their folkways and their acts furnish a start on a way to remedy the acknowledged shambles of our culture.

When a mob of students rips open and occupies some campus edifice, these adults applaud because the kids are really telling people what's the matter.

When, then, these criminal minors demand "amnesty" as the price, or part of the price, for evacuating a building held, or for releasing faculty hostages, the adults-in-years-but jubilantly concur with the latter-day and a-moral American doctrine that youth is sacred and beyond the law.

The educational philosophy of permissiveness which became the home indulgence of liberal-intellectual parents seemed to validate young America's sense of unlimited license and immunity to penalty. After all, a child of eighteen who has been schooled by the half-method of all-carrot-and-no-stick and who has experienced the same method of upbringing in his home cannot be expected to change his unbalanced sense of "justice" overnight and on reaching the university campus.

There, too, however, the LIE philosophy prevailed in a way that was different but no less ineffective. The university had once been a community of scholars that embodied a philosophy of reasonable men settling all controversy by reason and discussion. But it was not able to adjust its ideals to fit a non-scholarly mob of kids who reacted like hoodlums to their first encounter with authority, compulsory courses, arbitrary bureaucratic procedures and the necessity of doing work that was boring and that made it hard to stay in school.

The best and brightest and most dedicated faculty members couldn't communicate with such people. They tried and are trying. Why do they fail?

The radical activists won't listen to them.

Many others cannot even hear.

They continue to be loudly deaf.

And that, of course, is where the "generation gap" opens and widens.

You cannot decently make anybody listen without listening to them, in turn. The perpetual bellow of youngsters often, and in many instances, constantly, provides no open time for anybody else. So, listening to them becomes, for even patient adults, an absurd and soon an abandoned effort. It is like trying to get into a panel show on TV which you are watching in your living room. No matter how cogent, telling, useful and even sympathetic your comments might be, the people arguing on the big, blue vacuum keep talking and you couldn't reach them if you rammed your head into the set.

From the faculty viewpoint, too, there will often have been no way to screen applicants for a selection of potential scholars. In some state universities, any high school diplomate often has to be admitted and that, with recent, extraneous concerns of institutions of higher learning, has made communication even in basic English impossible. Millions of freshmen don't even have a command of basic English.

One can listen long and make endless notes of what is heard from young America and often not find a word or a statement that is even sane. Some "educators" are even willing to insanity!

Students who demand the right to hire and fire professors and to state the curriculum, get heard and even are allowed, now, in some schools, leeway in those matters! But that isn't education. What young people would enjoy studying is not what they need to know to become mature or even to be acceptable as voters.

And when they demand—when they even *get* "black studies," the faculty providing them will have yielded to a pressure that itself has no meaning. Is there a color line in knowledge?

And where this "black study" compulsion is rooted in the idea that any such impossible separation of courses by color will ameliorate the black student's intolerable position, it is as mistaken as any idea can be. For, if there are special subjects about Negroes that will improve their social situation, such as their history, or sound anthropological or psychological information, such studies should be for *whites*. It is the honkies who are racists and desperately need that sort of "black studies."

The students who demand admission without requisite qualification, promotion without grades or examination and graduation without proof of achievement are asking a similar and unreal permissiveness. They are asking to be granted educational kudos and status without being in the least bit educated.

That is merely a nonnegotiable response to a non-demand. Even at Oxford, which is often cited as an affirmation of this nonsense, final exams have to be passed to prove the student did the work even if he was free to skip lectures and free of constant testing.

Oh, we listen.

But they don't.

Indeed, they don't listen to what they say, themselves. If they did, they'd be appalled.

For they'd hear these nothings. They'd catch the endless sound of their lingo and realize they were talking pot-rock gibberish, the babble of social and political scientists or their doubly inane, non-deductions.

What's the meaning of a "meaningful relationship"?

How do you "politicize" masses of minors in institutions that cannot permit even majorities to determine what will be taught, or who will teach it, since the individuals in that majority haven't yet found out what or who they won't accept?

The inmates cannot run the asylum, I think.

And who can know "Where it's at" with no idea of where it was or where it's going? Not anybody.

What, again, is a "non-student"? Everybody else, I assume; people not studying or people who never studied. Why do students find association with them of use? It's worth is, by definition, limited to activities that have nothing to do with any concern of *students*.

We who listen hear all this.

After the trial of the "Chicago Seven," that four-way abortion, I even listened to a long session of several of those sentenced fur-heads at the apartment of one of them. Slowly, their just deserts occurred to me. They ought to be set on some vacant island, supplied with whatever necessities, comforts and luxuries they could name, save one, and left there, alone. All seven. The one item forbidden to them would be—an audience.

They would always have six potential listeners in their group. But never a mike would be handed to them, nor a camera set in their purlieus and not one added living being (except, say, for generosity's sake, a weekly hour, each, with a groupie volunteer) would ever know what they said. They would have to listen to what *they* said and *only* to that. No books or magazines or papers, no TV or radio would add fragrance to their discussions. And, that way, in time, they really might hear what they do say.

Nothing.

The party line of a dead and always preposterous political doctrine. All, spouted with the uplifting and inspirational effect of a stuck hi-fi record.

They coined the term, "put on." It fits like a beetle's carapace, like the air in a jug.

Perhaps they will shut up and stop setting fire to public and private edifices before they start a counter-sound from the righteousness on the right that will drown them out and then destroy their bodies. Perhaps they will even discover they could be useful in this still-pretty-free USA. Perhaps.

Perhaps they'll see what a joke they are playing on themselves, what a black-humored joke. For how hilarious it would be, while they lasted, if they should actually achieve the revolutionary education their dreams are curdled with! Imagine them, then, leaving the campus, holders of degrees in preselected subjects taught by whim-chosen professors with, as they put it at Harvard, "more poetry" in their lectures and classes less "boring." "Safe, now, in the wide, wide world," as the seniors sing it at my alma mater.

Safe, my eye! Unemployable. Unfit, even, to chop wood for a commune. Certain to be jailed within hours, too. Or, if they got over the border into one of their idolized leftist paradises, executed in ten free steps, maximum.

Meantime, how joyless they are! How somber! How ashamed, really! How furtive and ignorant, how, under pressure, ass-kissing! What a sad affair in youth! And no wonder, for people who talk so much, so loudly, about realities of which they are invincibly ignorant and will not study, poor dopes! Pitiful people, lost forever in hundreds of thousands but still sure they were born luminous, still convinced their noise is light for themselves and others.

You better listen to the kids. Maybe they have something to say!

They do, indeed, they do!

The trouble is, the kids haven't listened yet. That's where the message is direly needed.

A recent phenomenon has elicited both styles of that adult "better listen" bleat—and done that in a new and exceedingly dubious way.

It began with the Woodstock–White Lake mass rock and Aquarian affair. There have been many more since that one, though they were usually smaller.

From all ends of the nation came some four hundred thousand kids who had the time and money to travel to the site. There, they became a near-incredible thing, a multitude in the rain and mud that remained relatively "orderly" for three days—to the amazement of the police—while suffering great privations owing to lack of food, water, shelter, toilets, everything needed for the most modest comfort and the most elementary sanitation.

When that event was over a great many TV emirs, editorial writers, columnists, magazine article fabricators, noted speakers, grandiose politicians and others reacted with that fatuous glow I have described. These were, all, adults. They listened and were enthralled.

I listened, too.

I understood the phenomenon, I believe. The absence of riot, of pig-baiting, bloodied heads and clouds of tear gas was due to two factors. The first was that, for once, the "kids" were treated in the manner they had expected to be treated, and were treated in their homes and high schools: permissively. The other was that, when hundreds of thou-

sands of them had assembled, they were able to see that
"power" was inherent in numbers, an entrancing experience
and one they exercised with what they regarded as love, as
relating, as grooving and communicating.

Of course, statistical probability operated among them,
even so. And their beautiful peace was achieved owing to aid
by some genuine grownups.

Adult society rushed medical aid to the masses. People in
the area went to work supplying water and food. Law was
suspended for the entire period. Roads were blocked for
miles and for days. Ninety per cent of the multitude are said
to have smoked marijuana and all hard and dangerous drugs
were peddled openly. Thousands were injured and given
medical care. Hundreds freaked out on bad trips and experts from New York City tended them. The music clanged
on, even though myriads could barely hear at their distance.
Their feet kneaded urine and feces into the deepening muck.
A baby was born. Three of them died: a bad trip that was
fatal, a burst appendix, a boy run over by a tractor.

Nobody knows how many of the people present went
home with what toll from ensuing ills, mononucleosis, flu,
colds, VD, drug prostration, a heroin habit, what not.

They went about nude and had sex relations in public.
There, and in the other festivals, too. Personally, I have no
objection to nudity or to sexual relations in public but I must
note the law customarily frowns on such "candid" or "amaz-
ingly loving" antics.

Tens of thousands of men and women, in prison at that
time, had been arrested, tried and sentenced for doing exactly what most of those kids did at those festivals. The
"beauty" of it all was owing to the absence of what our
society calls legality. And while I do not agree with the
justice of some of the laws that were suspended during these
carnivals I cannot but feel that, if an effort to enforce existing

laws had been made, the love and peace of any of these assemblies would have turned into war, the kid-fabricated slough into abattoir.

Two conclusions seem valid:

First, that when near a half-million kids are allowed to make a mockery of the law and then told it was a beautiful scene, the telling in no way enhances their appreciation of law itself. Rather, it reinforces their contempt for any justice and pads their sense of being immune to penalty.

Second, and this is predictive, there are going to be many more of these assemblies. And sooner or later as such multitudes spill into out-of-bounds property, pull up their fence posts for fires, raid gardens for food, expose neighborhood children to orgy—as some outraged adults will call it —there are going to be reactions opposite to those so far on record. Not just a few people will become infuriated, as has been the case so far, but many. And when that happens, the agencies of law enforcement will be summoned and will do their duty, which is law enforcement.

Wonderment at such scenes will not be absolute, or even near that, indefinitely. The 89-percenters will act.

Those multitudes who are currently broadcasting hysterical and infamous lies in an effort to stop simple sex education in our schools, for example, are not going to take a kindly view of public sex education by exhibition. And the vast adult majority of Americans who take a dim view of kids using speed and H, not to mention grass, is also going to realize that permitting youths in tens or hundreds of thousands to do such things openly and without prevention or penalty isn't congruent with their sense of propriety.

Even the young antipathy for cleanliness is a somewhat understandable response to our adult passion for numberless products that are supposed to give us scented breath, surgically immaculate skin and to stop sweat (though the products usually do not and cannot furnish their advertised results). But the juvenile reaction of going dirty, affected by so many kids, may, in some next musical event, result in an epidemic which might reveal yet another flaw in the new dogma of anti-dogma. That likely possibility may alone lead to public demur at proposals for more of these scenes.

They bemuse me and so does the warmth accorded the participants by so many adults. It is, so far, a negatively-based warmth, one that stemmed from the mere fact that these people did not commit more and worse crimes.

And I am bemused by the cause that brought the masses, hard rock.

The initial event was treated as if something holy were involved, an assemblage like the one which produced the miracle of the loaves and fishes, or the effect on some of a Hindu mass collected to gather darshan from a revered speaker, to glean his glory scraped off on all present. It was seen as Moslems see the Mecca hadj.

But no such lofty if vain motive was magnet to these youngsters.

They came to be pot-stoned and undergo mass hypnosis by the rhythm of electronically-amplified guitars and by voices that whined and bleated their common self-pity and their vacuous dreams. They came to join in a depersonalized, drugged fornication called love and relating, and when the happening ended, what had happened that was of value?

Had they gained some precious, new particle of that identity they say they are in search of?

Of course not. They had gone through a tranced experience of identity-loss, *loss* in a mob that is per se without that priceless human possession, a thing that destroys self-awareness. They sought identity-loss by drugged escape from even that actual scene, loss of self in a common submergence of personality such as occurs among victims of evangelical fundamentalism and is called catatonia, echolalia, or hysteria, with the saved often rolling between pews in sexual ecstasy.

So, in thinking of this new young scene I am not very much impressed by the attribution of beauty to the participants, or by the idea that they "said" something I could listen to with enlightenment. If they were forbearing in spite of the rain and the mud they were perhaps forbearing because they were high and because of the permissiveness that let them laugh at equality under law, and because they were there to blow their minds and did so, unaware that when the mind is blown, identity goes with it.

Secular evangelism by rock bands is, I feel, no greater evidence of character or love or beauty or truth than the evangelical sort.

And even though I enjoy some rock music, in moderation and modulated, even though I am pro-sexual and object neither to nudity nor public copulation, I am not able to reconcile the extralegal permissiveness which must obtain to make these scenes possible and I do not believe it is worth the implicit risks taken to gain the meager fun and the collective thrill of the affairs. That never was a road to real salvation. And mud is no place to fuck.

The first such festivals were also cited by outsiders, by some adults and by participants as demonstrations of youth "power."

It is their favorite word . . . power.

Hair power, flower power, youth power, political power, power.

And by that perpetual reiteration they protest too much. They imagine these dizzy, absurd or vicious assertions of power to be liberating, new to the annals of mob psychology and "good." What emerges is the *impotence* of these power-claimants and power-seekers. Their self-styled impotence is not what they claim, the result of oppression by the system.

It is real and their own and it rises from their abdication of the only humane means and routes to genuine power, the hard learning and intelligence and the discipline that, alone, enable the individual or group to own and administer any useful or constructive power, at all. They are all symbols for the mob's power, mindless, antihuman, self-destructive and socially ruinous.

So, I listen.

I agree with much of the bill of particulars youth draws up against the status quo. I always have agreed.

But, so far, I still have heard no sound, however faint, of any suggestion relating to my "hope," the great hope that has burgeoned in this century but is still invisible and inaudible to adults, while youth seems willfully even more blind and deaf. Man needs hope, and hope requires a grail, not a crusade for the sake of slaughtering infidels, that is people we disagree with.

Sometimes I feel it would be a good idea to change the voting age as a last possible means of arresting the rise of a mean-spirited yet hedonistic anarchy so widely displayed by this young generation.

They have been demanding the vote be given at age eighteen. They *fight* at eighteen, don't they?

There's one of their hundreds of major non sequiturs.

I have discussed others and a few more remain to be noted before I turn to my hope.

The notion that, as technological man and his attendant, dreadful problems grow daily more complex, the ballot should be tendered to people younger than twenty-one, people three years less knowledgeable and less mature, if the word be allowed that gross elasticity, is appalling.

What we ought to do to save anything of value or even potential value, is, maybe, to raise the voting age to thirty.

9. The So-Far Silent Majority

It has been my assumption up to this point that the reader would understand or, at least, infer my views of the "silent majority." This group may not remain silent in the future since some members are already organizing to meet activist forays with counterpunches. However, the very great majority of students and of nonstudent youth is not what the rebel minority calls "involved," another word the amorphous-minded harp on.

Statistics here are unreliable. One reads that the hard-core activists are at most 2 per cent of student youth. That figure is expanded often because the noninvolved people tend to get involved with the mutineers on many occasions.

However, it is clear that most people under thirty are not engaged in rebellious activities or in mutinous plotting. Most of them are going to class or to work or to war with a view of ultimately stepping into the present system and becoming members of its establishment, and important members if they are college graduates. They are still, essentially, squares.

The "subculture" of the "involved" effects them only to a minor degree. They often follow modified forms of its hair

and garb styles. They can somewhat relate to the rebels because they are of an unripe, suggestible age and attend the
same schools. The far-outs affect the cultural habits, ideas,
manners and dress of others because they design the trend
of current costumes of youth—as they always did. But the
silents are not "politicized," not brainwashed by sociological
jargon, not removed from reality by drugs or dedicated to
the cult of meaningful relationships by unisex or omnisexuality.

Students intending to be doctors, lawyers, scientists and
technologists (as well as student-athletes, or jocks) ignore or
even deplore the activist uproar and ideologies. However, a
larger number of these squares than hitherto have been
persuaded to prepare for careers in education or social service and even in conservation so as to stand clear of the
mainline establishment. Still, the majority plans to follow in
father's footsteps, more or less, and the differences are not
of a revolutionary nature or degree.

This means that they more or less propose to perpetuate the
values, life styles, mores, traditions, sins, evils and hypocrisies
that both the mutineers and I find abominable. So these
young Americans are not merely a dead loss but a drag in
embryo form on the future.

To applaud, as they sometimes do, the New Left, the
SDS, the militant blacks, the activists just because they tick
off faults and then do something—anything—of imagined
effectiveness, leaves me cold.

It is like applauding a man who sees a house on fire, and
then, aware that some sort of action is necessary, begins
throwing buckets of gasoline into the conflagration without,
however, noting what effect that has—and without noticing,
also, the infants and children at the upstairs windows who
need to be saved and who could be if their activities were of
a more valuable sort.

To fail to notice the fire, or to see it and refuse to do a

thing, is the posture of this silent majority. Compared to them, the activists are at least more busy even if they are utterly mad.

The squares have not even made the minimal first step. They think things are generally okay, as surveys have proven over and over. They are young men and women, boys and girls, who will vote as their parents did, join the same clubs, attend the same churches, share the same prejudices, enjoy the same sports and the same TV programs, read the same house organs and slanted journals, belong to the same political party, eat the same sorts of food, drive the same car-equivalents with the same lack of skill, marry the same status-oriented spouses and so conform, in sum, in their second thirty years to whatever may be the standards then, that mom and dad would have lived by, then.

They are "with it . . . *as is.*

And even though they are entirely sound about the excesses in bijouterie, sackcloth-and-ashes garments, political idiocy, mutiny, crime and sniveling demands for amnesty of the troubled troublemakers, viewing it all as inane, dangerous, hateful, disturbing, infantile and pointless, that insight is in no way hopeful.

Indeed, the complacency it reveals indicates they really are, at least in one sense, more stupid than the activists, since these are, as they themselves tediously point out, the "brightest" of the lot, kids with the highest IQ's who get, if they want, the best grades, come from the top families, etc. The great square majority has an opportunity its generations of predecessors lacked. For, while it can and does find the rabid antics and the ritual sociologicisms of the rebels without appeal and even a cause for wrath, this greatest group never, or at least rarely, looks into the source of the chaos among the brassy few.

The silents are in the best place of us all to "listen," in

school with the people who say nobody listens to them—and they cannot help hearing something. Not liking what they hear—and see—the square millions fail to ask if there is any reason behind what is, itself, reasonless.

In my burning-home analogy, this majority sees the fire and sees that the active young doers are kooky to think gasoline-throwing is an act of sanity. But they usually do not see the children in the windows upstairs or hear their cries for help. They don't turn in a fire alarm because they think somebody else did that, or will do so, or because it's not their house and they don't want to get involved.

If they try to do anything about the fire, they feel, cops will arrive with the fire engines and you may be picked up on suspicion of arson or owing to propinquity amidst the gas brigade.

Even if they happen to hear the tots' cries or see them in the smoke-shrouded windows, they don't do anything. Rescue, if it is to be managed, is the problem of others trained for the job. They are training for different work.

This behavior is very common, nowadays. Dozens can watch a woman stabbed to death over a half-hour period and not even phone the police. Tens of thousands can stare at a poor devil on a skyscraper ledge and *urge* him with one voice to jump, even though the sorry creature is still in two minds about suicide.

There is today a thousand times as much of this non-involvement in USA as there is involvement of any sort, idiot or real. Psychologists have made tests which, they say, prove the strange inhumanity and discompassion of this age is owing to a fear of looking foolish, of offering help where it isn't needed and where the offerer would be laughed at by others standing around and passing by—others who, of course, aren't about to help, either, not being saps.

I think this theory is only partially correct. I suspect

the horror numbness of most of us, nowadays, is owing to a deeper and more degenerate factor than a fear of being humiliated. Presently, I shall explain that.

Meanwhile, however, and owing to likely comments and queries by readers of this much of the treatise, I have a need to enter a few more notes on our silent majority.

What has been stupefying about mom and pop and what still is, can be summed up as the *righteousness and self-righteousness* with which they have supported their perverse, mistaken, bigoted and infamous beliefs.

The silent majority of youth openly asserts its aim to hold the same perfidious convictions with the same righteousness and self-righteousness, forever.

This is hopeless.

Curiously enough, the New Left, SDS, activist gaggle holds different and false positions exactly as righteously and as self-righteously.

They are, psychologically, but a mirror-image of loathed parents and hated adults.

Seen in perspective, both extremes are identical at the core.

Neither generation has values worth a damn, neither one can think, neither has the education essential for any appropriate reform of our society and nation. Both are adamant, arbitrary, close-minded, ignorant, foolish and exactly equal in their assurance of rectitude.

"Momism" is a domestic form of totalitarianism.

The activists are totalitarian in the same manner and degree. But a member of the Students for a Democratic Society isn't any more aware of his antidemocratic stance than a member of the Daughters of the American Revolution is aware of the fascistic essence of her feelings of superiority.

And though most members of the third, or Scientific Establishment are presumably liberal and classify themselves as that, their concept of objectivity breeds a lofty irresponsi-

bility toward social uses of their findings. They have not yet
seen that while it is vital that they be without responsibility
for what they discover and learn in order to proceed with
discovery and learning, intellectual freedom cannot be rationally extended to include a human right of irresponsibility for
human misuses of their knowledge. That is elitist, unfree
and the snob's way. They, and they alone, have the ability
to evaluate the consequences of applications of science, and
when they fail to do that, they abandon the future of all
men to incompetents.

Their action is therefore limited to the uses of freedom
solely for scientific work. As citizens, they reject involvement
and society becomes the victim of their default, which then
becomes authoritarian by their deliberate self-exclusion, their
default as human beings.

If the greater educational effect of the LIE is to turn out
masses who cannot possibly understand a technological society,
the smaller section of academe that teaches science turns
out its bachelors, masters and doctors in the belief that they
have no obligation to do anything about what they have
learned even where its use is relevant to mankind.

Many of the members of our silent majority take these
half-blank courses—that aren't even offered by the LIE to
their students.

Since the Scientific Establishment, though antitotalitarian
in its special realm, has generally been aloof where its
authority is necessary for a free society, and since the LIE
graduates are scientific morons, it is clear that, in my view,
nobody is educating anybody in a truly relevant manner and
neither the young nor their elders have any plan for relevant
education.

Two non-cultures with no lines of communication and opposite aims cannot long coexist.

That a LIE education is adequate is a myth.

That a scientific education is adequate, while it includes default from social duty, is a tragedy.

That a few among the activist LIE students have rebelled to any point is the proof of their cultural illiteracy.

That the silent majority not only fail to see even what the rebels see, and that they yet imagine they are as well educated as the mutineers, defines our national lack of any sense of learning.

It shows why there can be very, very few educated men and women in the country. It is even possible there are none sufficiently educated to put forward workable suggestions for the social changes and technological revisions that must be made to allow man to survive.

If, however, there are any Americans with an education sufficient for useful criticism and constructive proposals, one fact about them will be sure: they will be *self-educated*, truly educated and in this only possible way:

They will be people who learned how to learn and to want to learn—people who did not stop learning when they received their degree or degrees—people who developed a means of evaluation of all knowledge in order to determine what they had to understand for useful thought—people who, then, knew what they did not know and learned that if necessary—people who also realized that what they'd been taught in universities and graduate schools was being altered, modified, discarded and replaced by improved knowledge, constantly, and so, people who never ceased the effort of keeping abreast of changes in areas of knowledge they regarded as vital—people who, in the current idiom, could tell it like it is and tell all of it that mattered, because they knew how it was and so, people who, alone, could tell it like it ought to be . . . if anyone can.

Perhaps they could.

Certainly, nobody else could.

But if such people exist they are rare.

Even if they do not exist, it would be possible for us to obtain the equivalent contribution.

By evaluating various groups of the part-educated we could select the most learned and open-minded specialists. Committees of such people, on which every major realm of cogent knowledge was represented by articulate and outstanding members, could pool, assess and reassess their collective learning, first, to provide the sum of knowledge all members would initially lack so that, next, they could learn it to examine the quandaries, problems, disasters-in-the-making, social follies, injustices and all else that needs study and change, with a view of finding all the elements of problems and, then, the best means to solutions. No solutions are possible until the given problems are that completely understood.

This process, of course, is abhorrent to all who believe in what we call democracy and self-government and who still have the deluded conviction that we *are* free and self-governed.

The LIE with one voice would call it dictatorship. The LIE cannot face a rule by a reality principle though it swallows irrational, sociopolitical dictatorship without gagging.

Business, industry, commerce, the military would violently repudiate the concept: it would shatter their beloved abuses of power.

The rebel youths would sneer and rage at it.

The silent and noninvolved majority who intend to continue the celebration of status quo would reject it.

To Americans, rule by any "elite" is tyranny even where "elite" means, simply, informed and capable.

But, in effect, that is how we are being governed already, with one difference: the elite decision-makers are intellectually unqualified politicians or people chosen by such elected politicians who lack the sense to make the appointments. And when the specialists, scientists, engineers and others who are called on to advise the witless heads of government do give their informed counsel, it is generally ignored. In any event, such counsel is often that of "experts" whose jobs and positions prejudice their judgments.

Most presidents, politicians, congressmen, statesmen, governors and all other elected and appointed administrators in America do not even know the difference between a scientist and an applied scientist. Thus they generally consult an engineer, even a member of the Army Corps of Engineers, on projects that should be designed (or forbidden) by ecologists, not heavy-machine operators with a vested interest in empire-building and river-ruin.

Nobody's in charge.

Nobody realizes that, where the action is.

So we are being half-educated or quarter-educated or one-fiftieth-educated and we still imagine we can know what we are doing.

Sometimes, I don't blame the kids who choose rock-to-love-stoned escape as an unconscious means not so much to rebel as to stand clear, for a bit, from the certain future, in a pleasant, if deliberately chosen and short-term now.

Perhaps they will be able to look back with a quasi-happy smile at a time when they at least made it with a few girls in the rain, mud and music, too drugged to realize what else was in the mud and too scared of tomorrow to blow their minds clear because things outside the amplifier range were already so hideous that tomorrow wasn't anything to dream of or work for.

But that's sentiment.

I understand what I deplore, here.

I want them to stand up with lucid minds.

And I want them to quit telling me how much they know

that I won't listen to, because they don't know enough to do
any damned good, talking, even, at their age.

They *could* know.

That is what power *is*.

10.   The Relatively More Knowledgeable Generation

Another, as vast an area of non-thought, is common to the young generation.

It calls itself, rightly, "the first TV generation." But it also claims to be relatively more knowledgeable than the generation of its parents. This claim is based on its TV experience. And here, again, the question of logic is involved.

For, in my innumerable dialogues with young people and in the millions of words I've heard and read about them and their motives, nature, behavior, relatively better-informed state and so on, I haven't found any evidence that their claim of superiority in knowing is valid.

Television, after all, is the very sound, sight and soul of the loathed establishment and system. It is a thousand times as "commercial" as "educational." And, while it is true that tots weaned on TV grow up spending more hours in front of the blue tube than in front of teachers, it is by no means demonstrable that the youth-long experience provides them even with comparatively more knowledge than their sires had.

What the young mean, undoubtedly, is that, owing to TV, they have seen and heard about more places, people, events and "facts" than any prior generation. But their single source, a kaleidoscope of sounds and images, is, at best, a sampling of sifted and censored reality. What is shown is what is acceptable to the establishment and system. The great bulk of it, furthermore, is whatever the hucksters find most attractive to the largest audience.

The TV generation knows what Bangkok looks like, and Moscow, or New Delhi, and it has listened to leaders of the nation, but it has done this in a spotty and unevaluated manner. Relationships, real worth and much hard information relevant to the exhibits do not appear. Programs are either slanted toward those ideals and images that suit the square world, or else the rest is proffered in bits, utterly incomplete and at odd hours. Television is, then, largely an animated photograph album with sound, prefabricated, precensored, and incoherent, and 90 per cent of it is designed to entertain slobs.

The value system on which programming is based does not aim to educate but to move goods and sell services. Often its intent is to prohibit learning. And it is not, really, possible to garner from TV many facts, and the real information needed to evaluate those facts, as it is possible from other sources, or, actually, one other source, reading.

Primary, secondary and college-level education certainly have not changed so greatly in the past three decades that they furnish support for the "relatively greater knowledge" young adults claim to have. That, in fact, is their *complaint* about education, its lack of change. And the TV networks do not attempt to bridge that gap. Where they display unappetizing "documentaries" it is with reluctance and as a sop to those who protest TV's will to be and remain as much as possible what it is, commercial. The influence of "ratings" on programming determines its nature and content almost entirely so that what the TV generation learns from the medium is not what is needed for knowing, but what the most viewers want to watch.

More than once, I've challenged highly-placed TV executives (who, of course, attentively view the programs), to tell me what they have learned from the medium that I, who rarely pay any attention to TV but who read a great deal, have missed. There is, of course, no sensible response to the challenge. Television addicts can say I failed to catch a few symphony concerts they caught. But these could have been heard by means of a record player and heard, furthermore, when I had the time and was in the mood to listen.

Several additional and major aspects of TV are ignored by those who act as its apologists. These are aspects not even visible to the young millions who assume that the medium has made them more knowing.

One such lethal flaw is its time factor. An individual learns at his own speed. And though any "knowledge" presented on TV is geared to slow-studies in order merely to have any audience whatever, the medium prohibits time-arrest for re-examination. That, in itself, precludes all genuine study. One either assimilates what one can of the running sound and picture or one does not. But one cannot, without elaborate technical gadgets, stop the action or the words to reassess them. Where a datum is offered, it is therefore assimilated as is, or not, and opportunity for checking by re-examination or re-evaluation is nil. Miss a word, look away and you have gotten a wrong impression or maybe lost the ball game. That is not true of print and reading.

Coherent thinking about TV data is, then, not possible. One's essential pace is not possible. Appraisal is not possible. Comparison is not possible. Furthermore, the medium is interrupted every ten minutes or so for a "commercial" which, in effect, literally prohibits any viewer from continuous, concentrated thought or assimilation. It even appears that TV, with radio, has destroyed the attention span of the majority of Americans.

Several educators have told me that is the case for nearly all primary students and most students beyond that level. The attention span of young Americans is now said to be about ten minutes, which is the minimal average for dogs. Educators and social scientists have, of course, no "control group" for comparison. They did not think to measure the pre-electronic attention span of young human beings. But people who could read a book, magazine or newspaper for an hour, uninterruptedly, were numerous in my youth. They were, I suspect, people for whom reading was both a pleasure and a means to learn.

The boastful TV generation also fails to realize that it is the *second* electronic generation. For it was preceded by a "radio generation" which, of course, was furnished with the identical flow of non-stopability and the same interruptions at equally short intervals. Young America, then, ought to recognize that its parents were as intellectually sabotaged as themselves by that similar medium.

For TV is, after all, simply two-dimensional radio. One now sees what one also hears, but the visual addition alters the effect of radio only by intensifying what became a national addiction in the early twenties. Not one generation, then, but nearly two generations have been reared by media that competed, and won the advantage in spent time, with school and that also cut down the general attention span, identically.

Those who defend or who advocate TV as a source of knowledge have rarely attempted to present their case *on* TV or radio. The media they use are magazines and books and that is true of the most extravagant defender of electronic media, McLuhan. Live, on TV, he seems to me not to know what he is going to say (or to write and print, for that matter) until he has spoken (or written). And after either such performance, he leaves the impossible interpretation to the viewer, hearer or reader.

If his so-called theories have caused wide interest it is not owing to their logic or to the newly coined terms in which he makes his apology. People who watch TV and who use it to baby-sit young America and keep schoolkids from bothering anybody, would like to think they and their tube-transfixed offspring were doing some useful thing like gaining information from a "cool" medium that McLuhan says will replace the "hot, linear" medium of print.

This stuff is, of course, erudite bullshit. Neither medium is hot or cold compared with the other. And to imagine "the medium is the message," as I've said elsewhere, is as ridiculous as to imagine, "the violin is the music." People who find such facile sophistries acceptable are, plainly, brainless people in search of an alibi for their mindless addiction to and uses of TV.

To claim to be relatively more knowledgeable than prior generations, and claim also to be the first TV generation, overlooks the just noted fact that the TV generation was preceded by a "radio generation" as hooked as they are. When the same people assault the current system and establishment, they ignore the fact that it was the work of people as radio-fixated as they are TV-stoned. Their abused parents were deprived of learning and logic by being affixed to a one-dimensional medium which TV merely doubles, without in any way improving itself as a means for learning. The impact may be squared or cubed, but the magnification of nothing remains zero.

Television, again, is entertainment, at least for those who can be entertained by minimal-information, maximally "non-controversial" programs, or by endless violence here regarded as not controversial. Their habit of being everlastingly diverted by TV palpably corrupts the youthful rebels. When, for example, they exhort their fellow students (as cited for Harvard) to strike "because courses are dull," because "classes are a bore" and in order to get "more poetry in lectures," one sees they have come to expect learning to be entertaining above all, an attitude nonexistent in pre-electronic times and a very silly one, too.

Real learning, to be sure, is vastly exciting and so, "entertaining" in that sense. All teachers and professors of worth try to give the learning process that quality. But when students demand that classes be arranged so as not to be boring and lectures be "more poetic" they reveal an inability to be excited by *learning itself*. They show a capacity to learn only if they are primarily diverted!

Nobody in the LIE or elsewhere seems able, at this late date, even to "ask the right questions" where TV is concerned. Thus the main, current discussion of TV is based on the question of its endless and near-perpetual exploitation of violence. The question asked is, "Does violence on TV have any effect on the watching tens of millions of tots, preteens, teen-agers and others?" This astigmatic query is bandied about by all sorts of self-styled experts. It is not even apt.

For to phrase it that way is analogous to asking if TV commercials have any effect.

If TV commercials did not have a tremendous effect in results of a measurable sort, there wouldn't be any or they'd be changed. So any question about the effect or non-effect of the interminable TV violence is witless.

The proper question goes, *Is the endless and immeasurable effect of TV violence to make TV viewers more violent or to "sublimate" their "natural" violence?* Even in that form, the question subsumes that people are naturally violent and that watching mayhem on TV may sublimate a merely presumed, innate and grisly aspect of human beings. Man is violent but is it natural?

To one who is sure, as is this author, that man's violence rises from a perversion of his nature, even that improved question is not accurate. Here, however, one must also observe that what is called "TV violence" is not in any way a reprise of actual violence. The vocal agony, the visible suffering of victims, the shock of actual mayhem are not TV's bag. That what it does show is dreadful, painful, cruel, perverted, lethal isn't part of the exhibition. The gutshot actors are only actors, acting shot. Even a newsreel display of wounded soldiers in real war is not accompanied by their torment, its sights, sounds and duration.

So TV "violence" is at most a brief, semi-image of the results of reality. Oftener, by far, it is simply play-acting. If the results of the real thing were visible on the tube and audible on the sound track, America's tube-toadies would puke, faint, suffer heart attacks and mob the studios in protest.

Television "violence," in sum, is not that, but a false representation of the truth. What effect has *that*, then?

When, at Columbia, the police were called to remove the militants from occupied buildings, it was the cops who were most astonished. What astonished them was that the young mutineers against whom they were forced to use violence were dumfounded. The students, in effect, either assumed they were immune to physical assault no matter what they did or else they imagined that being clobbered wouldn't hurt. Perhaps they imagined both. But their amazement at the fact that violence was used against *them* when they resisted violently, and their shock on finding that it hurt to be clobbered and to bleed, was still more shocking to the police, who had no other means to carry out their orders.

That is one possible answer to a cogent query about TV violence. On the tube it doesn't hurt the viewer. The TV generation didn't expect it would happen to, or hurt, them. Which appalled the cops.

The dimension TV does not and cannot supply is that of *experience*, of *feeling*. One sees. One hears. One never feels —or even often wants to feel. If TV did magically furnish feeling with the two-dimensional show it would, again, be thrown out of every American house in a day. Who could bear dying a hundred times, suffering a hundred mutilations, being bashed, torn, scalded, raped, mugged, clubbed, gutshot and a thousand more similar weekly injuries? Who could bear a real soap opera in the home? Or almost any comedian without a script? Nobody.

Books and other printed matter don't furnish direct feeling either, but they are very often means to it as well as to all that TV omits in order to be accepted, graphic images of real emotion. They therefore offer what TV cannot, in its news, its documentaries and its massive bulk of non-news and non- or anti-enlightenment that is entertainment for dolts. Relatively few citizens could face in person the sights and sounds involved over a period of days in the actual torturing of even one captive American by an enemy. Some few people find the ceaseless *vapidity* of TV shows almost as agonizing.

In that, again, TV is like the movies which, with a feature, a comedy and a newsreel, also occupied weekly hours of the older citizens of the land. The shift from movie theaters and radio to TV was, in fact, merely an intensification and a multiplication of the regular experience of the generation our rebel youths condemn. Instead of assuming TV has relatively broadened their minds, made them comparatively more knowledgeable, given them a cause for brag, young America ought, surely, to note that its unbearable, hypocritical parents had experienced the same thing and nearly as constantly, in movies-plus-radio. That awareness might at least cause them to wonder how much of the damage done to the people they so vehemently malign was done to them by their equally degrading and more-accessible TV.

The thought that their parents' background was so nearly like their own in this vast and empty area, that their own history is one that has merely been exposed to a movie projector attached to an old radio is worth the study by our young.

There are other such uncontemplated verities, here.

Educational channels and cultural specials rarely have large audiences, even when an educational channel is available or when one network, as one occasionally does, sets aside an hour in some week to present a truly "informative" documentary. For TV is limited, as are public schools, to that area of such education as underaverage Christians permit. The network people, like schoolteachers, have no stomach for authentic, clinical examinations of, for example, politicians, big business, religion, sex, pressure groups or even moms.

Perhaps one reason youth is so anti-industry and anti-system is, simply, that it has been stewed in the TV medium so long and borne with such myriads of odious commercials that it unconsciously revolts against the cost in unconsciously (but willingly) paid for interminable, poor, fragmented diversion by tube-squatting. If so, the young rebels still will have little concept of the real vices of system-establishment against which they now rise in anger. Theirs will then be a wrath owing to surfeit of which they are unaware. That situation suggests an explanation of much of the gist of the young giant killers' special hostilities. As I have said, they don't know anything about technology or want to learn: that ignorant rejection may rise from the just-suggested, uncon-

scious resentments at the infinite hard-sell of the technico-
logical products hawked on TV.

Television is two-dimensional and incapable of supplying
feeling, is unable, in a clearer term, to furnish any complete
knowledge whatsoever. One may get vistas of all the foreign
cities of earth on TV but these cannot add up to the value
of a single visit in person to an alien metropolis.

Learning, in general, is only in part listening to, reading
about and seeing others do what is being taught. One learns
best and most and fastest by doing. But that act of doing as a
means to early learning must be supervised by a human being
who will be able to discern each learner's particular per-
plexities, hang-ups, and the private causes of his errors, a
highly subtle process which involves the emotions of teacher
and pupil as much as it involves demonstration and student-
trial, error and retrial. Television, of course, has no such
way to "teach," at all. Even teaching machines are not able to
catch nuances of the student-user that any able teacher could.

Television at best simply offers a mass of disconnected,
partial and unrelated information which may or may not be
understood even as intended, which cannot be played back,
which is always subject to the massive restrictions of the
self-elected censors who emasculate the minds of our society,
and, finally, which cannot possibly supply experience to any
viewer. Its faults as a learning medium are great; its failure
as that is implicit.

When one thinks that more than 98 per cent of the adult
Americans cannot even say what Communism *is* and when
one sets that perhaps fatal datum alongside the fact that these
same people spend four or five TV hours a day, one is
forced to acknowledge that TV hasn't done even a microscopic job in teaching something it talks about and exhibits
virtually every day! If TV did contribute even meagerly to
knowledge, that specific ignorance would be impossible.

Like the newspapers, radio and most magazines of wide circulation, TV is a business enterprise and exists to make money. Even its news is only part of the whole news—the part judged to have widest appeal. Through exclusion of news with narrower appeal, what we read in papers, hear on radio and see-hear on TV is what has maximum impact, sock, attention-grab for the biggest numbers. Since, in a depraved or an infantile society, this will largely be word of events that stir the simple-minded, news that's often dramatic or violent, or local and trivial compared to important goings-on, one can say unequivocally that TV is the opposite of educational and gives a distorted image even of news.

One need only clock a week of a regular news period to see how the great mass of it is of that sort. International, national and the local news is heavily dedicated to strife, war, storms, fires, disasters, starvation, strike scenes, mobs in action, alarming weapons and their effects, hijacked planes, holdups, bank robberies, murders, vice-raids and accidents, including on the-scene stares at the crumpled cars and the blood-soaked dead or the injured being pulled free of the metal shambles.

The impression left is that violence is universal and predominant. It is so greatly such an impression that a recent report of a survey made for *Look* magazine revealed that middle-class and upper middle-class whites in exclusively white areas of a large American city are twice as frightened over the likelihood of violence as the ghetto people where the rate of violence is double and an event the far-less-scared slum dwellers frequently witness and of which they often are the victims. From that sort of study it is necessary to infer that reality, even where violence is concerned, *diminishes* panic in relation to the unreality of its TV and press reports, which are the usual and often or even nearly always the only middle-class measures of the menace of violence.

The crassness and banality of the programs is equal in offensiveness to the violence. The quality of American life as represented in nearly all situation dramas and comedies, in the endless serials about families, in the soap operas of radio now transferred to two dimensions on TV, the debasement of males by wives and daughters displayed as brighter, the tedium and tawdriness, the appeal to every inferior and cheap lust for titillation, the absence of any higher sort of value or any sign of common sense, let alone of wisdom, the tawdry motivations and piss ant aims and goals have permeated the American public for almost fifty years, now, and TV is merely the most compelling medium for that avalanche of degraded crap.

How, I have asked myself since the first radio programs made rude imbeciles of millions, can a person have so little to do and so meager an interest in self-and-being to bear, let alone to want to spend, even five seconds every day in front of this Niagara of honey-shit? Time was when, if you called a friend at the American dinner hour the friend might reply, "Amos and Andy," and hang up. That began it all and I lost those friends. Now, millions don't answer the phone if Dopey Daddy is on the tube. And the viewers actually overwhelm city sewers because they wait to micturate for the commercial break so as not to miss a moment of Corporal Jerk.

Occasionally, I have an appointment with TV. Usually, I miss it simply owing to the fact that what I am doing is too interesting to permit my constant attention on the time of day or night. Once in a while, if I am in the mood and if the tube happens to suit it, I watch a game of football for a while, or a golf tournament. But I do that with two handy pairs of spectacles in order to read during the commercials for I cannot bear one in fifty on a first showing and to bear even an acceptable commercial twice is not possible for me. Who would tolerate the recitation of a dull verse by a half-wit, at augmented volume, over and over? His mother?

Perhaps people over sixty-five, as I am, are lucky. Some of us, at least, learned to read so well that by the time radio took over the American home we were immune. The world of print is at least millions of times as wide and great as that of radio and TV. The written word can and does supply all that is feebly and occasionally if ever furnished by TV, plus all the opportunity to experience in one's special, imaginative terms and pace ten thousand, basic realities TV cannot even exhibit.

Television, however, is everybody's same, canned, prefab substitute for private imagination.

Television is America's baby-sitter even if a live baby-sitter is employed, for she or he watches it with the kids.

When, then, young critics speak of the depersonalization of our present way of life, their missing but sought identity, their sense of alienation, I think I know what they are talking about. Their parents had the same empty feelings before them, though less intensely. Both groups were of the radio-movie or TV generations. Both reached college age so deprived of actual experience and so robbed of a chance to exercise their own imagination of vicarious experience, so stuffed with sounds and scenes that no imaginative living being would want to experience, that neither one has much direct orientation and both have been pounded into compliance by messages of the unreal media. Pickled fantasies intended to get one sort of notice:

BUY! OWN! CONSUME! NOTHING DOWN AND YEARS TO PAY! GAIN STATUS! DIAMONDS! NEW CARS! A BETTER HOME! ELECTRIC HEATING! LET YOUR KIDS' POSSESSION SHOW YOUR TRUE WORTH AS POP AND MOM!

That's the net effect and whosoever asserts he or she is a

member of the first TV generation, and does so with pride, cannot attribute his other woe of alienation or of missing identity to anyone but himself, a lost gnat in the swarming viewers. Nor can such a person claim to be relatively more knowledgeable than members of previous generations.

For the children who spend more time watching TV than they do in school—most youngsters, now—will have been brainwashed, not educated. They will not know who they are because they spent the time in which they could have found that out, in but one place, watching a pallid, cacophonic, hash, and an endless lie about man, and men-and-women, about children, the world and about the supreme value of *things,* beer, soap, cars and other blood-fatiguers.

These will also be the students who did twelve years of homework with the radio turned on.

They have become, then, young persons who cannot even hear the music for their dancing, unless it is tuned up to a super-homework volume that makes them permanently deaf.

The X million tots now sitting in front of twenty-one million color sets will also be getting their balls and ovaries battered by radiation and their genes curdled, unless pop or mom has had the set checked, for this sinister spin-off is true of sets of all makes and a particular set's radio flux is not ascertainable without special measurement. How many, then, have been measured for radiation dosage?

How many genes are being savaged? To savage how many unborn?

Nobody can say.

People who would not dream of weaning their tots on hog slops are, en masse, weaning young America, year after year (and they have been for fifty years, with no hope of a halt) on this everlasting swill that is designed for a no-brain.

I am, of course, aware that many undergraduates have come to a point where they ignore TV or, at least, rarely suck at its sticky, lethal teats, the three or four it has on its usual pig-belly.

But I am also aware that these are people eighteen or over and it is too late to recover from what was, to them, a daily and massive feeding of intellectual diet-cola and brain fillers that do not nourish. The establishment and system have already desensitized them, taken away their very living from their formative years, alienated them from experience and destroyed their sense of responsibility.

The atrocity that is TV merely begins here.

For it does not just occupy children and young people, it destroys childhood and youth. Its teency-weency merits, what minor, occasional gobbets of information it imparts, are tuned out by the viewers. They watch the network shows and there, no choice exists since what NBC finds profitable is shortly swiped and displayed by ABC and CBS. The "educational" channels don't interest kids. School is like that. There's little money for those programs, in any case, so they lack the grandiose-garbage appeal of network productions.

Transfixed, agog, stupefied and paralyzed, young America glares in red-eyed afternoons and evenings at this trap and its claptrap bait. The children cannot live in their daily five hours of asphyxia. They are not outdoors. They hardly move. Their minds are masturbated. Meantime, their values are buggered till all they prize is what the commercials tell them is of value. They cannot exercise. Their parents set them in front of this colossal toy, this constant candy-maker, and the child dies. His grown corpse thinks it is knowledgeable and cannot know it is empty of wisdom and stuffed with shit.

It is, proponents say, free. So are prisons, all other penitentiaries. No Louis ever charged people for chopping off their heads, either. And TV is not free, of course. Added to the cost of the sets as they deteriorate and are traded in, and the price of electric current, is that measureless cost of lost existence. The big toy also produces toys, all the expensive child-molesters sold by hammering commercials to the dead sitters.

Perhaps that is the final analysis of our situation, our massive mediocrity, our absence of value-judgement, our violence against nature and ourselves. We have become toy-users and nothing real is very visible to us. If seen, it is seen as worthless unless it is a toy or can be dealt with in toy-fashion, for small, nasty kicks.

Time was when young people had few toys and the majority of them made their playthings out of whatever came to hand. This is one way imagination grows and whoever has a dwarfed imagination has lost all that is human, all that makes man other than animal. Murder, observed without involvement, as I said, is entertainment. It has got to be, since that is what so often beguiles us on TV. War is fun and so are burning buildings and shot soldiers, right? Of course! For, on TV, these are just great.

And all this, without effort! A tot who builds castles in the sand is on the way to maturity. One who but twists a dial to sit before pictures of castles and miniature people in flickering, blotched snapshots of castles stormed and castles bombed, Martian castles, even, and men on the moon, has not even come close to the feat of building one's own castle on the beach and peopling it with imagined knights, ladies or martians. For imagination, all man owns that beasts lack, is a do-it-yourself enterprise. It cannot be developed by a gadget built to erase the need of imagining and that, by corrupting truth. Compassion, empathy, sympathy, even motivation to think, learn and merely to be, die in the blue-lit gas chambers where TV is the brain's cyanide and the body's toxic agent of atrophy.

Perhaps we cannot survive TV. Certainly, all efforts to

"improve" the medium have scarcely thinned out the pistols. Maybe we will be wise enough, or sufficiently desperate, in time, to do the one thing that could save us: abandon television. For would it not be preferable to give that up when keeping it means we are giving up, generation by generation, our young people and then, producing the haunted, mentally ill, tormented and lifeless adults these become? How long can we bear capture by this Thing and by the things it produces, that avalanche of mind-and-muscle slayers.

Time was when boys mowed lawns and girls washed dishes. Then boys cut grass (more or less) with motorized mowers. Machines took over the dirty dishes. Next, they had seats on the mowers. Now, electric lights so the lawn can be cut in the cool of night. The air-conditioned farm tractor is here and the lawn mower can't be far off. The plastic lawn has arrived. And sister's dishes aren't even washed, today; they are disposable. So, as a consequence, is sister, along with brother. The saved labor gives them that much more time to watch TV and so become the more deranged and dis-oriented, physically weaker and generally cheapened, dis-individuated, decerebrate.

It is not any wonder that youth is in revolt. And it is even less wonder that the revolt itself is as savage as it is pointless, and violent, too, since violence is fun and nobody really gets hurt that way. Indeed, TV doesn't allow violence to hurt, must I repeat. How often do you see in the putrescent phosphors some person crawling about while his knees pull out his intentines? And when do these candid bits about the birth of babies show monsters issuing from dying mothers? Nothing's real. Everything is to play with.

The message of the medium is clear. Illusion is real, reality, a myth.

That is the state of this "more knowledgeable" generation. Its sense of its intellectual superiority rises from its ignorance of the nature of truth and the genuine uses of mind. It lives in a people-world, a LIE world, unaware of the laws of nature, the governance, a world of artifacts. And it has no logics, no accurate dreams, no wisdom or, as it so often admits, no aim or goal. It only knows what it does not want: *all that is real.*

11. The Sex Revolution

People who dip into books and, particularly, those who hunt for the "dirty" passages, may spot this chapter in the index and hurriedly leaf to these words.

They will be disappointed.

Of course, there is a "sex revolution" in progress. There usually is. The current one is an extension of the revolution of my youth. In those days, too, we were involved in trying to emancipate woman from her secondary status. We were endeavoring to make human sexuality clean and natural, that is, free it of the avalanche of shit our predecessors had sent down on it.

We knew, even then, that this filthy tonnage had been shoveled so the priest-caste could throw into the believers that fear, that sense of shame, which would oblige them to accept dominion by the God-surrogates and pay tribute to them for any sex-related act, beginning with christening, continuing as chastity, and from there to holy matrimony and its churchly mandate of fidelity. We weren't about to accept that artifice and stigma as God's noose held by holy men.

We did not, I think, so much protest sexual "roles" as do
the young of this time. We wanted "equality" for females
but we had not yet clearly seen how beggared man and
woman had become, or would, in the service of the modern,
industrial, mass-producing state. We still felt that a woman
ought to occupy a home if she could, have children and
tend them. We also assumed that a father would play his
part in such a home, washing dishes till the kids could, and
being present in fact and act as a symbol of a proper male
in order that his sons and daughters could grow up with
some idea of that role. Virginity and chastity were optional.

When the technological and urbal society obliged dad to
become a domestic cop-out, or gave him that excuse, on
which he generally acted, mom had, often, to try to represent
the mature female and the absent male too. She couldn't.
And wherever she thought she made that effort, momism
emerged.

Least of all did we anticipate the swiftly ensuing situation
in which the kids, junior and sis, teen-aged or even pre-
teens, would be tendered great or even major powers of
decision in the family. This was unimaginable and even
though the vipers of the under-thirty lot have plainly suffered
this incredible affliction, it still is hard for me to visualize as
an experience in what still was called a "home."

But, evidently, it happened.

Discipline, alone, is the route to self-discipline. The example of a sexually mature, on-hand, active male and female,
alone, serves to start boys and girls toward a suitable maturity.
But, plainly, a minimum of several hundreds of thousands
of them, nowadays, are proof of parental cop-out, or else, in
some way, juveniles permitted to cop out on growing up.
Any teen-age boy or girl who has, at that time, been able to
superimpose his or her will, in any family matter, over

contrary or even unfinished decisions of his or her parents, has learned something that absolutely is not true.

"Permissiveness," however, was the style of LIE education and the ruling creed of Dr. Spock, so, evidently, lots of young people were reared and educated to imagine there was no penalty for wrong-doing but only reward for doing right. The fact that the wrong-doer in the real world catches pure hell, and that the doer of the right gets nothing for merely being right and only such compensation as the deed may earn, escaped these kids.

Now, they are basing their sex revolution, like the rest, on that sort of experience and disastrous inference.

Their rejection of the standard male role is sound enough. It was the role presented by Sinclair Lewis in *Babbit*. Television has further defiled the father-image in USA till he is a nothing. The historic female role as subservient and secondary was infamous, too. So is the present standard role that presents woman as a pretty, empty-headed lure. When woman is seen as a member of the sex that, alone, is sensitive, has taste and appreciates the arts—while the male is devoid of such qualities, that pair of roles is fishy, also.

Variations on role-designs as vacuous could be extended to infinity. Rebellion against them is, merely, evidence of some potential for sanity.

But though the potential is still displayed, the sanity remains obscure. There is one over-all reason:

No culture and no society, no group or human tribe ever did define the human sex roles satisfactorily.

Nobody knows what they should be.

Or, if anybody ever knew, the knowledge has either been lost or wouldn't do for life in modern civilization.

The young revolutionaries don't even recognize where the confusion begins.

Every human being is born with a sexual appetite and the capability of its gratification. Until we establish the "right" mores for dealing with that natural, universal (and, if you believe in God, "God-given") hunger, we shall not be considering what roles are suitable for anybody, of any age or either sex.

No discussion amongst the sex revolutionaries of this matter is worth notice and, indeed, one hears virtually none. The time limit of their revolt is about a week. Perhaps fruitful reflection on how to bring up sexual tots is not rationally possible for people who, as tots, were reared as if sexless. Certainly, what our innate drives, organs and capacities tend to suggest as proper is some sort of adult behavior that would produce kids who would be social outcasts and either secretive little odd-balls or else get their parents jailed.

When any large group of adults is ready to deal with this situation in some relevant and open manner that, then, will not produce eccentrics or jail-risks, I shall be willing to say the opportunity has come for seeking appropriate sexual roles through vast and perhaps frequently mistaken experiments, live and in color and the flesh. Till then, sex revolutions will be merely the uncomfortable antics of persons who are, in effect, too senile for answers of any worth.

Such visible reactions as we have are, at best, sad and productive of sorrow and, often, disgraceful, disgusting or mad.

"Unisex," for example, is merely another exhibit of the common rebound of under-thirty rebels—a mere ricochet into a pose that is opposite to the posture they imagine prevalent, among adults or, possible prevalent as "ideal" but hypo-critically evaded in act.

Unisex is biologically ridiculous.

To achieve it as nearly as people can is to hide and deny one basic clue to identity. If one imagines one's self as a person but neither male nor female, one has lost himself or herself, even as a human.

Unisex is, then, an effort to cop out on sex. It is an attempt, in the imagination, to become at once, both neuter and a hermaphrodite.

The strident programs of militant members of the woman's liberation movement are just as silly. If the assigned role is mistaken, and we can agree that it is, why do they try to change that by efforts devoted exclusively at shifting the male role? Where the screaming sex need is reconciliation, how come these loud lepers figure to be cleansed by communicating their diagnosed disease?

Again, suppose the sex revolution creates a society in which, as one lass described her local scene, "A boy can tell any girl he'd like to make it with her; if she says 'No,' he won't be hurt; lots of other girls will say 'Yes.'"

Or, suppose it leads to what is an evidently growing pastime of adults and youths, too: wife-swapping and date-switching?

Will either of the above mores provide us all with the ideal roles? What if the girl who says "No" is the only girl the asking boy wanted to fuck? Is this problem solved, his role perfect?

As for swapping, does that make the roles clearer? From all I read and hear, this cuddlesome effort is a "club" enterprise mainly. But how would any one couple go about finding four or ten or maybe twenty other couples who would enable an even exchange, or a different swap of even worth, or any swap in which each of the involved individuals would find all the members of the opposite sex in the chosen group sexually desirable, even sexually bearable?

If, in effect, sex revolution merely reduces the human worth of the sexual act with another to that level at which partners need only be opposite-sexed, has that achieved anything role-wise? Supposing all the people involved in both the above situations, the asking boys and refusing-or-accepting girls, or the swapped partners, *were* of identical worth, as bed-companions, what would *that* indicate. It would indicate either that the criteria for an ideal lay are physical and mechanical or that the partners had been mass-manufactured to operate like motorized sump pumps.

Indeed, the ground rule for exchanging mates and dates assumes such robot people: there must be no personal attachment, no emotion, no discrimination or value-sense in the action. It is conducted for kicks, exclusively, and therefore a depersonalized game.

A revolutionary code that included such a regulation would be impossible for those under-thirties who so widely state they are in search of an identity. But, then, they often are searching for that in crowds, in street-mobs, at rock festivals and by collective ideologies or by being stoned—means to achieve impersonality, dis-individuation and identification with an amorphous whole.

Girl-haired boys are a principal symptom of such seeking.

They wear long hair, they say, as a sign of their individuality and of their right to do as they please in the matter of coiffure. But they all do the same thing, which negates that alleged aim. If that's pointed out, they say long hair on males is an emblem of a group that opposes false values of short-haired men. Actually, it makes them look like girls, is all: you have to see the ass of such asses to distinguish their sex. And as a badge of revolt, it's pretty poor.

Employers in the square world who refuse to hire these tress-dangled males, or refuse them welfare funds, also stand on the matter of civil rights—their own right to hire or reject people by any regulations they choose. They're paying, aren't they? But that is risky in these days when a huge legal aid society defends as "civil rights" all sorts of people and concepts which, if conceded by courts often ignore the rights of the employer. The employer is compelled, unless he wins his point, to hire a man with a fright-wig, or feed him on the public funds. An employer may even be compelled to hire a black because he is black or a female because she is not male.

Fine. Egalitarianism is beautiful. Race prejudice is filthy. Prejudice against paying women less for doing what had been a man's job, is unjust. But in all these matters of equality we may be in trouble, indeed, we are in trouble wherever we demand identical-everything for all people on the mere grounds that they are people. These grounds have long been the region the LIE has most honored and most extended.

Equal opportunity, is all that the most just man (or God) can honorably use for an ethic in the matter. A man and woman are not equal. If a woman holds a job for which a man would get more, that is unjust providing she does it as well as he. If a trade, skill or job can be done identically well by any one among numbers of people, they surely have a right to form a union. But does the union have a right to set conditions that make employer's payroll so great, by featherbedding and other such arbitrary and infantile union regulations that the employer cannot continue to build houses? Does organized labor have a right to deprive the entire public of economies and of technical improvements by insisting on medieval craftsmanship?

Or, what of human beings whose professional work is of a kind that not one other living human being can do? Ought they to form unions like the people who are replaceable? Can you justly force an author to join a union of playwrights, movie writers, TV scripters and then, to pay dues to support the inept or lazy and even cease writing altogether, if the union calls a strike, for the benefit of getting higher wages, not for the irreplaceable union member but the interchangeable hacks?

What I am trying to explain is the liberal-intellectual confusion about freedom and individualism. An illustration will help. Suppose Shakespeare had lived under the current and law-enforced rules now covering his kind of work. Suppose the guild he had to join went on strike to get more dough for members who were doing scripts for stand-up country fair comics and changing Punch-and-Judy show routines for local audience gags. These underpaid members would, plainly, be exchangeable. Any one of dozens could do as well as any other.

Shakespeare has to strike, too. Also, he has to pony up his savings for the war chest of the strikers. The actor's guild will join in—no crossing of picket lines of playwrights. The Bard's next drama was only an idea. His advance dissolves in assessments to support the strike. And this happens several times in the Bard's career so the world, as a result, will get along without *Hamlet, Macbeth* and *Lear*. The Bard couldn't get a production. He was broke. He didn't write in those intervals because he had to eat so he shoveled snow in London, or worked in stables in Devon, doing whatever came to hand that would feed Anne, himself, a few dependents.

This is not just a far-out fantasy about the LIE concept of civil rights and organized labor, it is what the LIE has *done*. It shows how the people who call themselves defenders of freedom and individuality abuse both ideals for the collective and only-alleged "good." The result, among the under-thirty people, is their visible lack of a mere means to know what is meant by liberty, or by individuality.

The hair scene is one evidence of their funk.

A couple of years ago, as longer locks became fashionable,

I dubiously followed the fad after family urging and until my own hair fell below my long nose. And I found I had become a menace to myself and the public. A slight shift of wind could blind me when I was crossing a street or driving a car. It was evident that the boys with bobbed hair were worse off—limited to tunnel vision. Moreover, in a recent half-year we lived in an area that was hippie-thick. Most of the many girl-boys let their locks go uncombed and unwashed. They were liabilities even on bicycles. The further fact that they were dandruff-prone, louse-attractive and stank was a civil right, maybe; but their diminished vision was hazardous to everybody.

In innumerable jobs they would be, like hair-careless females, unemployable, and for their own good. For females with similar (though this is unusual) heedless care of their tresses are often scalped by home appliances. Industrial machines are out for all such.

"Hair power" is, then, enhanced weakness. Who would be able to engage in real combat if he were liable to instant occlusion of vision? Who can sensibly engage in ordinary games and sports with the constant threat of sudden sightlessness? What hair-impaired nut could compete with men who are sensible enough to avoid that deliberate handicap? And who, in this violent, urban society, is ready, as a male, for self-defense or the defense of others, women, children, when the first move that shakes him will also put out his eyes?

Adding a beard or mustache to retract the girl-coiffure-sign doesn't relieve the one with such additives of his deliberate self-limitation. So, even if "hair" is thought a badge of revolt against the system and a password for rebel recognition, it also identifies the brothers as witless, self-endangered and a potential menace to anybody and everybody who expects their public behavior to be competent. The net effect, as "protest" of "individuals" who imagine this form reveals their rejection of the square mores, is absurd. The un-barbered boys have used a trick that is so regimented it means nothing—except that the boys look like girls, are filthy or else waste time.

Any such applicant should be refused work, or free meals, but not on the grounds of a right to let his locks grow long and fly free, which he has. But inasmuch as he cannot cross streets, or drive cars, go near machinery or mingle with crowds where he will bump into others because he cannot see them and they may be on crutches, old, or small, these are grounds for his rejection.

Not bathing as a mark of revolt against a society (that is, admittedly, insane about "cleanliness") is a folly of the same order. Filthiness invites disease and endangers all who are exposed to these two-sexed, unwashed pest-mongers. Since they will surely imagine they are also trying to make *sex* clean, their clotted clothes and mud-shod feet will conceal that ideal from rational and reasonably bathed people.

Many of those gambits are mini-martyrdoms and partake of that madness in proportion to their degree of self-inflicted damage. The syndrome peaks at immolation. But very few who have used gasoline and a match to emphasize a point got any message across. Those who managed, among them, numerous saints by their assortments of total masochism, spread sadism amongst their followers that has lasted for centuries and still continues. The martyr is the jumbo-sized child who never stopped screaming, "I won't play!" and, "I'll kill myself!" in the vicious belief that such threats of temporal or eternal non-participation would compel every-body to do his will.

It doesn't. A decently reared six-year-old ought to be past that sort of infantilism, but a million or more Americans haven't passed that emotional period, even at thirty.

There is a great deal of confusion amongst them; and there appears to be about as much amongst professors and the whole LIE membership over the difference between rebellion and temper tantrum. The current "sex revolution" is fecund of examples of tantrum, by symbol and act, by cop-out and by its extreme form, but even there, in reverse, this way:

A thunderingly huge part of the under-thirty lot, squares and rebels, acts from the idiot premise that *we* have doomed *them* by nuclear holocaust or ecological erasure. They are killing us, so to speak, in that manner, and ahead of the vent. Only a part of those mass-murderers by projection believes they will be included among the dead of their *a priori* slaughter. This dream is put forth constantly as an alibi for any and every headless or heartless act of mayhem, self-ruin or personal indulgence that youth engages in and so often attempts to justify that way.

By imagining that everybody over thirty in USA made the first A-bomb (and has made all the ensuing nuclear stockpiles apparently), they can really crucify us—though not the USSR, and by assuming our industrial efforts have sentenced all of us over thirty, and perhaps them, the innocents, to imminent extinction, they can get two colossal cracks at us, they think. Aside from the fact that the first notion is utterly specious and that, had USA not been first with a nuke, they'd be lying in Red graves, we aged sinners have lived as long as or longer than any of them in that "shadow of the bomb," which they ignore. There are other flaws in those disreputable and snide fantasies. A quarter of a century has passed without any nuclear holocaust, for one thing, and they can no more rely definitely on such an event in their private future than they can on horoscopes, tea leaves, mossy trees or bull's guts.

That other event they certify will happen, and soon, and owing to Americans over thirty, also might happen, sometime.

If it does, it will be the fault of all mankind who uses or ever used goods and services that drew on the resources of earth and mauled the biosphere. The young will be among the major contributors, too. And inasmuch as all science cannot even guess the odds in the matter (though science should get on the ball and find them out), these blood-thirsty dreamers, who won't even study such irrelevancies as science, are unfit to discuss the matter.

The fact that they do, and then go around in wanton debauchery, like people during medieval plagues, suggests that cop-out, injustice and hypocrisy are not monopolized by the middle-aged.

Two things, each of which might happen, of which one is wholly under human management and the other, more probably avoidable than not and, either way man's shame or it's remedy by man are the imaginary sources of young censure—and excuse.

A man or woman who is human, mature, reasonable in some slight but basic way, will not panic over unreal, malignant prediction. All men have always lived under the liability of Armageddon. It never was, it is not, and probably will not be for thousands of years possible for anybody to affirm that the world today will exist tomorrow.

There is evidence that many events have endangered life on this planet. The facts suggest a recurrence is probable and might wipe out man. The astronauts brought back proof that the sun, apparently, erupted at least once and boiled rocks on the moon. The magnetic poles have switched repeatedly and another switch is about due—with certainly dire effects. For all any astronomer knows there may be a hunk of dense matter flying toward us that would shatter the earth on impact, a missile that hasn't been spotted, and may not be, till a few moments or hours before the catastrophe.

I could add many such "likely" or "possible" doomsday

items. The generations before mine used to imagine other kinds, as well, horrors not possible but believed by multitudes and so, their alibi for criminal, licentious and ridiculous behavior. People under thirty will, of course, reply that those old fears rose from superstitiousness, that the scientifically possible ones I suggest are "acts of God" and beyond human control, while the two fates that buy them are of another kind. They are (or will even be) man-engendered, man-triggered and man's own fault: the fault will be that of criminal scientists and technologists who acted with the tacit consent of all Americans over thirty (whom you will have thus accused of guilt-by-association, hardly fair in view of your demands for due process and of justice). But you'll conclude, anyhow, that these phantom Armageddons are different for being works of man, older types.

If, of course, man is part of nature, the "difference" doesn't exist. He had and has the chance to identify himself in that one, real manner and if he does, the nuclear threat will vanish and the ecological menace will be tackled, swiftly, and by a united effort of all people, since all contribute to the peril. The statistical chances that our present ecological state is already irreversibly lethal are small, and an *educated* guess would not see the situation as hopeless.

We should, as I keep saying, find out how we stand. But till we do, the juvenile Jeremiahs have no excuse for their pity-loaded prophecy. Moreover, no change in man's assorted cultures, national folkways or his commercial value-systems will be sensible till we learn what to do about the environment—knowledge that might cost a hundred billion and take years for an appraisal that would then indicate acts and priorities.

This base-line requires scientists. Its inevitability will become clear, perhaps while you are alive; and it is too bad you find science so "irrelevant." Otherwise, you'd be among the most-valuable types on earth, at that point where humanity had to face the job. As it is, you will not be able to help, your suggestions about social or political or any other change will remain what they are now, rabid but off target, uninformed, like the square suggestions.

If the learning of one species concerning nature and its laws is evaded, ignored or spottily exploited in the Red-free-everyway-way of the present—and if that ruins the habit for the species, nature will see it as a minor event. A single life-form tried to break the rules and became extinct, of course.

Your ancestors, including your parents, faced a dangerous and uncertain life in a more risky and less comprehensible environment. They invented extra hazards precisely as horrible as yours. They hadn't any hope of establishing a culture with any chance, whatever, of a stable future. Their nations rose and fell because they obeyed laws of gods and God that were irrelevant to ecological law.

You are, then, members of that *first* group of people who derived the only knowledge that supplies a *chance* to establish an open-ended future.

You are, the first young generation ever to have a reason to hope. That privilege is the greatest men ever had!

This is the simple conclusion drawn from ecological insight showing our current errors and how we can rectify them. The chances that we can do what no past people could supply a more transcendent cause for joy than mankind dreamed of, till now.

What does that mean about you?

First, if you still imagine the world is doomed by what men have already done here, you are obsolete.

Second, if you believe all-is-lost because mankind cannot or will not salvage himself you have made a judgment of your species that is, to say the least, untenable. You cannot prove that low opinion because no such proof is possible, now, or, perhaps, for centuries, irrespective of what men do about their nukes or environment, or do not do, for that matter.

You have unwittingly acknowledged you neither know nor want to learn the disciplines in which all the relevant data is found. You are not old enough at thirty, even if you intend to become a scientist or *are* one, to have accumulated and weighed the galaxies of information that prove the new hope. And if your education has been the liberal-intellectual fraud, you will not even be able to gain this information without a half-dozen more years of learning.

This means in sum that you are either:

(a) superstitious—and you are, in great numbers, you absurd astrologers;

(b) stupid;

(c) a sucker for the gospel of others and one who can get the Red religion or any other, without the least exertion of a self with a brain could be critical and could do its own evaluating; or,

(d) you are so arrogant your self-esteem is functionally schizophrenic and you show that in hysteria and panic.

All such human conditions are inferior.

Superstition is a bag for fools, nowadays. Stupidity, while common and irreversible, hasn't the prevalence your mutiny suggests.

Are you a sucker?

What's that?

Anybody who believes in "doing his own thing" is a potential monster. For one's "own thing" may well be an excuse for ignoring other people. It is often the slogan of the absolutely selfish and to use it that way is to be what one does, a *thing*.

A sucker, however, is a thing who is doing somebody else's thing. That is possible for a human animal who is already a thing. A thing can become a tool at work on somebody else's thing, and yet presume it is human and its thing is not second-hand.

One's own "thing" could, of course, conceivably be a work undertaken with benefit to somebody else, or to everybody. But I have observed many own-thing-doers, and noted them as parasitical free-loaders, dependent on their scorned elders, irresponsible for ideas or acts, intellectual quacks and minimal artists of life.

In any previous era, such rogues wouldn't have made it to age twenty-one.

Oh, they "knew" much less, you say.

But they knew how to be human to a degree beyond the state of a thing, that you haven't imagined, even.

I am aware of Vietnam, too, of other wars as possible, of the unfair draft, the defective enforcement of civil rights, our failure to help the blacks, of the even-more-hideous condition and nature of public "education," now, as compared with my times of pollution, the terrible irrelevance of the LIE, of looming nukes, the repellent roles standard for males and females in a vast portion of USA, and other aches, besides.

Those provocations are real, and great, and perhaps seem more burdensome than their far worse equivalents in all the past, because the irritated under-thirties feel ills are now more amenable to cure. But it is possible that these people are overconfident owing to an insubstantial notion that anything and everything is open to remedy, and quickly, because of a permissive childhood and their sense that candy must fall whenever you drop the (given) penny.

Can it also be that the media, and especially TV, imbued them with the belief that there's a pill for every pain and also for emotional anguish? Their degrading school experience taken with the spoiled-child-syndrome, doesn't completely account for their extensive cop-outs. But something happened to many which might be explained by their incredible exposure to a medium devoted to the sale of nostrums for instant relief.

In any event, the people who most conspicuously work at changing sex roles, by word and act, seem to have the least understanding of sex, itself. And to the degree sex is a "basic drive," I find them—as I've just discussed them in other connotations—too emotional, ignorant, lacking in reason and ungenerous for a task demanding reconciling features and not more hostile extremes.

Consider, for example, the present and growing fad of copping out by entering or setting up "communes." There, experimental sex roles are usually part of the program. But, again, what are the conscious motives of the act, and what, if it can be adduced, unconsciously promotes this self-defeating fugue?

Taking to the hills, mountains, forest or arroyo in commune-fashion is, to begin with, not only a renunciation of the dreadful world of civilization, but the self-removal of every such human unit as a potential asset in any effort to straighten things out. The alibi for that, of course, is their stereotype: the commune-folk will develop new ethics and lifeways which, later, somehow, in some form, will be valuable to the outside world.

Such presumptions are identical with and include those which posit imminent doom by bombs or by pollution and the one about the aftermath of the world which the militant Reds offer. Once the establishment and system are smashed (and they are, of course, *it*) some new and better idea of how to be boss and run the show will suddenly occur to them.

Why such childish daydreams are taken seriously even by people in junior high school, is hardly understandable. Whatever their calendar age, they're about seven, intellectually.

For nobody escapes or finds reality by moving into the woods.

Growing your own vegetables, cutting your own firewood, building your own house, caring for your own kids as amateur physicians and teachers, increases your and their risks and assures a net loss in nearly every important category of being for the would-be escapist.

I happen to be a trained woodsman and an authority on ocean survival. I have built my own house, boat, cut my wood and I've lived for months in a wilderness no human being had entered before, one far from doctors or even the nearest inhabited place; a Hudson Bay post.

When, then, I contemplate life in a commune, I do so with a solid basis for appraisal. As what a scientist-friend calls "a relatively nonvocational scientist," I have yet another set of criteria.

If that all-out h-war occurs, for example, no bomb-evading commune will long survive. Biological radio-magnification will get them, finally, even if the first effects and subsequent fall-out should skip them. If pollution writes finis to man, it will only be when the last men have consumed what remains, including whatever may be on hand in the remotest communes. More likely, the planet will run out of oxygen-adequate air, or something of that sort, an evenly distributed death, with communes no sanctuary.

There is too much rubbish and quackery in these commune plans and the "Everything" catalogues they live by. Certainly, for example, the packaged edibles in supermarkets are loaded with chemicals of a long-term effect not known and possibly harmful. But are the refugee types sure the grounds they plant will furnish less contaminated produce? Do they check it for pesticide content, now world-wide in varying amounts? For radioactivity, which fell and falls still, unevenly on the earth? Are they testing their water supply regularly for its bacteria count and for chemical toxins? These are universally present in some measure and subject to variability under numerous conditions, all, hard to measure and impossible to predict.

Have they, also, arranged a good carry-over adequate for a few years, in the event of extreme drought? Are they secure from floods of hitherto unrecorded magnitude? Tornadoes? (Nobody can be, of course) Earthquakes? Forest fire? Illness and epidemic transmitted by animal vectors? Or airborne? What about botulism, the flight of natural fertilizer and home canning? Trichinosis?

Such questions are meant to imply not merely the self-deception involved in the commune philosophy but another, the illusion of commune-inhabitants about freedom, self-reliance and all. What they have is gained by self-deceptions or by the genuine truth that, in any crisis the commune cannot handle, good old civilization is right there, to fall back on. And good old civilization, however invidious, polluted, paternalistic, law-freighted and authoritarian is likely to have a degree of creditable concern for helpless non-adults in the custody of parents or guardians whose way-of-life may well be, by any sensible and humane standard, a cause of jeopardy to the children.

In plainer terms, the communal scene may involve an irresponsibility that responsible people might or will undertake to accept, and that, with cause of an entirely rational and precisely demonstrable nature. The abandoned world will likely meddle, too, in ways outrageous in *my* view. But that is something else.

A sex revolution is certainly overdue, one based on human biology from birth and requiring large groups of adults to undertake a considerable number of experimental methods of child-rearing as it relates to inborn sexual realities. None of the past and prohibitive methods need retrial. The sex educational program should begin in laboratory colonies at the time of birth when urge appears. Some colonies should gratify sexual urges whenever they are expressed. If and when their tots take over by auto-erotic endeavors, that will furnish a datum. If and when the toddlers find that erotic gratification by others, providing they will have gone through a do-it-yourself phase, is more appealing, a division of modes in our colonies will, again, be required.

Who will be acceptable as a stimulator? Peers of both sexes? Currently, modern parents have reached a state where they are told to regard masturbation and the erotic play of tots with casual acceptance—though nobody has advised, in the parent-counseling media, that erotic games be started in the cradle. However, if Group B or C or 17 gets into the game of erotic peer-play, what should the parents do when, without a friend of the same age or either sex to play with, the kid asks mummie or dad to join in? Should they?

There is plenty of evidence among adults to support Freud's theory of an oedipal or an electra complex and that as the result of early, incestuous feelings, they have been repressed. If they were not repressed but acted out, would these causes of such neuroses exist? Freud didn't even wonder, so far as I recall.

Again, does any such series of child-rearing methods normally shift from (likely?) *homosexual and* heterosexual desires to the latter? And is that, then, absolute?

These children will, of course, enter schools at the usual age and sex education, there, will proceed along the various experimental lines employed by the several colonies. Every other physical skill and capacity is trained in public school so the pupils can ultimately learn to read, do problems, commit things to memory and even play guitars. No current program of sex education includes this same "learning by doing" technique—and even plans for learning from diagrams and plastic models of genitalia are being sturdily resisted at this time.

However, if "libido" is anywhere near the important drive many psychologists believe it to be (and most people discover it is, for themselves, too) an "education" in public schools that omits sexual learning by doing will create a vacuum or barrier or absence in the child's mind that will be in scale with the drive of the evaded subject. Children may never be conscious of that great gap. By the time most reach Grade One, in fact, they will doubtless know real teaching in the area is out and that they'll meet disapproval if they even bring up the topic.

But I have often surmised, and it may be true, that when *the* basic drive, or that a big one, is omitted, or even gingerly entered, in the curriculum, with wax models and nervous monologues, but no doing-to-learn, as is elsewhere routine, the thus deprived child may not really be educable to any degree in any realm. That, or else, his biological sense of reality may lead him and her to enough covert activity to let the small flame of libido flicker bravely until better days arrive.

In fact, it can be flatly stated that a child who has no sex education has been crippled, and the best vicarious sorts, I believe, are nearly as ineffectual as silence.

Such evidence as can be had fortifies that actually-obvious belief. The sexual permissiveness of a Summerhill, or of other trial-run imitations of that school, is suggestive of what I hold, even though the actual conditions, entrance-ages, cultural immolation required for a simple and sane experiment and the outside social mores the sadly released adolescents encounter are hampering factors too great for any sure conclusion.

There are many other unknowns. Some of the most able sex-researchers say there is no such experience as "vaginal orgasm." Others can give its anatomy and motor-patterns, along with the training-means to gain the ability and the

subjective effects of such orgasm in women sufficiently un-
inhibited to achieve more than a development of the essential muscles and, with them, blood and nerve supplies.
Who has the facts? A woman who never experienced vaginal
orgasm couldn't bear witness. And if the physical processes
and subjective reports of that event, as beyond any clitorally
induced climax, *are*, still, merely accessory to what they
limit as clitoral orgasm, how do they describe orgasms induced by erotic manipulation of other areas, nipples, the anal
passage and so on?

What *is*—and *isn't*—fact, here?

The palpable confusions and experimental contradictions
in this area need more work.

Communes, or mere activists who are actively revising
sex behavior by acting out opposition to the standard role
kinds, are not possibly engaged in their games in ways that
can produce hard information about sex roles even in direct,
erotic relationships.

The *reason* for "nature's invention of two sexes," as the late
and much lamented Joseph Wood Krutch pointed out, was,
simply, to accelerate evolution. Sex increased the ability of
life-forms to multiply at a rate higher than the pre-sexual two-
for-one pace. It permitted dozens of offspring for any pair,
even, millions—and that was the exponential factor in aid
of evolutionary acceleration.

The fact may seem currently pointless to a species suffering a cruel and lethal population explosion. But, at least,
it discloses a fundamental reason for two-sexed species and
that reason, in turn, seems to show at least adult homosexuality
as an aberration.

Sex roles for man still have to be discovered and pro-
mulgated in whatever their right way may be, a way in
which correct function is strongly suggested by human form.
Further, we *do* know that the earlier and oftener males

and females commence sexual activity the later into life their capability, desire and performance will continue, a not negligible matter.

If role-shifts you may be trying as mere revolt have any general value, I cannot imagine what the value might be. For I find it difficult to attribute to instinct an intelligent if occult drive which would now be preparing man and woman for either unisexual or omnisexual roles even if some approaching New Man is to manage the entire procedure of fertilization and fetal development in labs. (Add genetics to that method and it might be dandy!)

But the problem of parents for these flask-carried, anony-mous-donated-sperm-ovum-babies remains. Even in the USSR it was soon discovered that the original program for the institutional care and rearing of the young was no good and they are back on the family mandate plan. Rene Spaatz could have told them that error before so many young commies were victims of so much grief. And the "kibbutz" idea, that woman's lib now caterwauls about, is really day-care. The kids go home for a long late afternoon, evening and all-night life with father and mother, in Israel.

I think we can drop this discussion about here.

My main criticism of the under-thirty rebels where sex is concerned is their disregard of the thus-far optimum condition for child-rearing—at home, by parents. Until they start thinking of themselves as parents, whether they are or merely must expect to be, they will not have any useful ideas about man, society, systems, establishments or their own identities.

Their stark failure to consider the future at all is a sign of failure. For the future, the one they will be able to furnish their posterity, and what that implies they must do in the present, as planning, both as male and female, is the basis for all thinking that involves values. Perhaps they will

stop practicing sex with whatever variations they employ
and consider the purpose of it—evolution. Meantime, their
offspring, alive now or still some unripe cells in both males
and females, will not, probably, opt for a world with a
wrecked system and establishment, dominated by victorious
slobs who expect to get a vision of a grander way-of-life
by some arcane and spontaneous flash, amidst the ruins they
made.

The hardest act for most people of all ages and especially
for adults is to say, "I don't know."

Where that is the case the admission is essential to keep
the race alive. For what we do not know is what we then
know we perhaps or surely ought to find out.

I do not know the ideal or true roles for sexual behavior
at any age.

Neither do you.

But man needs that truth sorely. Without it we are not
really human.

12. Black

Compassion is one of man's greatest virtues.

To scorn a heart that bleeds in deserved sympathy for others is to beggar one's self. Yet when people with bleeding hearts have bloodless brains their agony will be augmented. Brainless attempts to alleviate the woe of others, their only sort, fail.

It is not possible for a white man to imagine what the life of a black one is like in this land.

It is very difficult for any man in an unpersecuted or peer group to have deep insight into those his group may consider inferior. I have often said that had I been born a Jew in America I would be dead by age twenty-one. So furious is my sense of injustice, I meant, that I could not have stood personally the anti-Semitism rampant in the USA. It would have led me to such lawless responses that I'd have been slain by the law—or suicided. My ego is that big, if you like.

Aware of that, I am aware of what I said earlier: I do not know what my stance on any current matter would be if I were young, today. I might be the solitary rebel I was.

I might be seizing a dean's office as any older reader might
who has or had some just indignation of spirit.

In my lucky life I've made a few close friends who were
Jewish. And I am aware of one truth about that circumstance.
No man or woman, no non-Jew, no WASP, nor super-white
nor any other person who has, however unconsciously, the
faintest whisper of prejudice against Jews will be able to
have one for a friend. Such persons may think they have,
but the Jews in those relationships will know better. It will
be they who make the noble concession that permits the
semblance of what cannot be real friendship.

When the Negro is considered this way, his plight becomes
so many times greater that it cannot be borne thoughtfully
by me. It is a thousand-fold increase of the plight of the
Jew in a merely somewhat free society.

But, like the unjust and terrible difficulty of the Jew in
an anti-Semitic milieu, the evil is in the others, not the Jew.
The black problem isn't black, then, but white—as the Kerner
Commission made so plain in its report to LBJ. The day
that report reached the White House was the day the President could and should have taken time on every TV network to point out that conclusion: every trouble and evil
attributed to the black man is caused by white people,
honkies, *you*, if you're white. It was not only a golden
opportunity but a national duty to stamp that documented
proof on the culpable faces of the offenders, us. LBJ flubbed
it.

So the terrible and perilous reality continues in its utterly
mistaken form and shape.

The more militant blacks resort in desperation to overt acts.
The harder the honkie clings to his prejudice the more
violent he makes the danger to himself, to what liberty remains in America, to whitey's hope and to his current rating
as ever-more-degenerate, in the very eyes of his own God.

Every paleface croak of "law 'n' order" is the sound of the croaker's sin. The black reality voids any honkie claim to Christianity, justice, rule by law, decency, humanity and even a clear title to American citizenship.

Never were any people more guilty and less willing to acknowledge their infamy and their responsibility for the consequences.

And never, I think, were men in similar straits farther from the proper course to pass through them.

The situation is neither new nor a monopoly of any one race or people. Pride in color exists everywhere and everywhere it exists it destroys all pride in man, the species. For whosoever deems himself superior by the event of being born one shade or another has judged other men inferior in his heart and mind; by that he has degraded man; and most of all, himself as a man.

What can be done here?

Nothing adequate can be done until the great majority of white bigots are shriven of their merciless and self-destroying views.

There was a time about fifty years ago when the great man under whom I began my study of biology, Edwin Grant Conklin, shocked honkie America by stating that in two centuries the "Negro problem" would vanish—vanish because, at the rate of black-white intermixing, no visibly black man, woman or child could be found in two hundred more years.

In a book I wrote long ago I suggested that mankind would never have peace or any hope until all the people on earth were "tea-colored." That merely reflected Dr. Conklin's statistics-supported bombshell.

When the first Supreme Court decision about equality was handed down, every editor in Dixie used my "tea-colored" prediction to show that I (claimed then, for Christ's sake! to be a liberal-intellectual) reflected their position: what the Yankee Commies demanded was racial merging, nigger-marriage, in sum.

Since then, of course, the infamous and biologically-bastard state laws against "miscegenation" have been constitutionally erased. However, the Dixicrat notion that I, or anybody, wanted to compel, somehow, blacks and whites to intermingle, wasn't my point and isn't that of anybody, even the LIE.

But the hellish illusion of "blood" as a reality continues. And though one can and must understand the final hopelessness that has given rise to black nationalism, militancy, separatism and the rest, it is, to me, a sad and regrettable blunder, an effort to achieve, by copying white bigotry, a separate way of life that is, again, merely unequal.

It would be interesting to learn how many honkies have how much of what they call "black blood." It is evident that few black Americans are "pure" blacks, of course, and that was the fact on which Professor Conklin based his prophecy. In a way, somewhat distant in past time but sure, *all* of us "Anglo-Saxons," all "Caucasians," have both Semitic and black blood. A part-black strain was brought to the British Isles by the Iberians. More came with the semitic Phoenicians and the black-mixed people of Carthage. No white man is pure white; the state is nonexistent. And all white men were probably black and black Africans, at the beginning.

In time, providing we manage to give each other time, it is sure we shall display our one species in tints too alike for racial distinctions. That wonderful era is not one I would compel, however, though wouldn't it be a happy affair if all white females volunteered to have a first baby by a black man before having another by a white spouse? Such a dreamlike and voluntary endeavor would at least mean the honkies had gotten the import of the True Word of their God.

But that social science fiction whim would be rejected by blacks, too, now, or in the near future.

It has only a sort of meaning, the implication that nobody of any one color can take pride in being human until color is not part of his ugly and self-besmirching idea of what is valuable as "human" and until the vanity and ignorant blunder of present appraisals is history.

Meanwhile, the bleeding hearts with bloodless brains . . .

I mean the Americans, especially, and of them, the young in particular, whose outrage at national injustice to black people is vast and valid but whose efforts to take ameliorative steps are usually senseless. . . .

Worst of those, I feel, is the youth crusade to take any and all blacks into colleges and schools, furnish them with special courses adjusted to their low educational levels (that honkie link in their heavy chains) provide special "black studies" (which, as I noted, don't exist for blacks and which, to come into existence, should be for whites and compulsory) and graduate them as educated at the university level.

Many blacks have snatched at that straw.

True, whitey is drowning them, that way. The straw is only a straw and waterlogged, as well.

Again, some religious denominations are beginning to pay money, as tribute, to militant blacks demanding it as compensation—as, for the donating honkies, conscience money.

God knows we need means to rescue our conscience. But money is only one such means, tens of billions are too little, and handing over fake trifles as if at gunpoint is neither a sign of brotherly love on the part of giver *or* receiver nor a way to exhibit faith or trust or even diminished bigotry.

Whitey can never touch this terrible white-sin with money and what it can do, alone.

To think remedy can even begin with material aid is not to think. As long as honkies hold their sense of superiority, nothing—better housing, better schools, higher education, equal treatment under the law, justice there, intermixed housing, integrated everything—will but achieve fractional good and also exacerbate the albino wickedness.

It is first and finally a matter of reconstruction of the midnight black heart of the so-called white man.

And here, more vividly than in the many other areas where young, rebel America intends to change the earth, the people who ought to hear what is true, that they call evil, aren't even much addressed, approached, appealed to or *known* by the New Left, by the LIE itself, or by the bleeding hearts with their bloodless brains, the well-intentioned fools.

The people who must be changed within, deeply, wholly are the American majority of middle-class and lower middle and lower-class white jerks. The majority, whose "silence" is louder than Krakatoa.

Until they see the Light they talk of in their holy churches (that are dark as the Pit in fact) nothing will give, nothing vital will be susceptible of improvement. With the middle mass and lesser stand a very considerable portion of the affluent Americans, too, those who deem they are upper-middle and upper class. The adamant enemy of hope is . . . this mostly Christian sod majority.

The material aid needed by poor black people will never achieve the necessary end, for it won't convert one white Christian to Christianity.

Any rich Jew can explain this, and perhaps this is why a disproportionate number of Jewish young people are activists and members of the New Left, just as they were of the Old

Left. All victims of prejudice who cannot escape from or remove the obscenity that pursues them without reason, all who find every honorable effort is doomed as years and centuries pass, are likely to grasp at other means, means that promise change because they promise to destroy the establishment and system under which they have suffered.

The Jews who were so numerous in the Old Left and so enthusiastic about Red Russia were, owing to their experience of disappointment in democracy, able to overlook the fact of anti-Semitism in that drear land, and even the Red pogroms, a still-current evidence of the persisting prejudice. A few Jews were big in the new tyranny, *so perhaps* . . . they said. Revolt, rebellion, revolution, mutiny . . . and to hell with the logic of the activists engaged, their aims or non-aims, so long as they are trying to sabotage what exists that is unbearable.

America's young activists *all* behave in somewhat that manner, as if they were genuine victims of the prejudice of older people. Indeed, they often believe they are casualties of a bigotry implicit in the American way of life, a willful bias that they imagine is grinding, crushing and misshaping them because they are young. Jews among them have a point, but it is a different one. The blacks have nothing but their Everest-high, rock-real point.

White Christians, Protestant and Catholic, have, after all, been the greatest oppressors in history and they are still oppressors.

Scores of millions of Americans even base their oppression of black citizens on their Holy Bible, on a phrase about "hewers of wood" and "drawers of water" written four thousand years ago and as filthy then as now.

Against such cruelty and obscenity it is "human" in a real if miserable and corrupt sense to implement violent hurts that rise from the viciousness of others with deeds of violence.

That such deeds may be erroneous or even that they have no aim but revenge will no longer seem relevant. For underneath any claim of noble intention in such acts lies that talion motive. When victims, real or fancied, have no means whatever for solving their situation, unjust or imagined as unjust, they can invent a war cry that sounds like glory but is meaningless, self-destructive and even suicidal. With it they can make a last, mad effort of retaliation.

The militant blacks . . .

And the vengefulness of the young activists . . .

Vengeance against what, in the latter case? Vengeance against everything that has sustained them, sustained and warped them in ways they cannot see, because they don't want to resemble the people who subsidized them, the same people they still, preposterously, expect to subsidize them, the poor, the oppressed on earth with material benefits that can be produced only by their detested sponsors.

Racism is a perfect example of revenge for the racist's own inferior self.

Men have been racists for tens and probably hundreds of thousands of years. Racism is our most visible trick for gaining what we think is status that is in fact its jettison.

To imagine racism can be eliminated from the infected majority of a nation in a year, a decade, even a century, as the LIE does, is to be ignorant of man's very essence.

What will it profit a black man if he be accorded the outer trappings of equality amongst white people who remain even a little racist? How will he even gain that appearance of being human when such people prevent its inner possibility? And what a terrible disappointment will be his if he is given the status badge—and that "education" which so many activists demand, a college "degree" based on "black studies" and on lower standards of admission and curriculum! What savage mockery will greet his entrance in the world beyond his specialized university environs, with a sheepskin taken from a goat and an "education" that is separate and unequal?

One can understand black men and women accepting this weasels' baiting because it offers something, or the seeming of something, that was not available before. But one cannot understand the leaky minds of honkie activists and "educators" who proffer such treachery as a means to meet a real obligation.

The black man's dilemma is not his but the honkie's. It is almost funny to note how lucidly and how unarguably the Kerner Commission documented that only basic fact—and how swiftly and completely it has been ignored . . . by the culprit majority, by the LIE, by the activist youths whose attempts to rectify the ageless and grisly condition, in view of reality, are like their faiths in magic, in mythic rites— the recourse of people who insist they can manage nature they once could not and now will not understand.

Great unions, the hundred million and more hearts that are racist whether they know it or not, even some black people and growing numbers of those, are being hardened in their terrible plight by all such foolish efforts of these would-be saviors.

They do not address the cause and the people who embody the cause of this colossal evil.

Their concept of what must be done to erase the sin is a measure of their minute minds. Bleeding hearts with bloodless brains, in truth.

Nobody listens?

Ah, you don't know who must, or that they are presently without ears to hear, or that until you do communicate with them and change their alleged souls absolutely, you will be talking to outer space.

The scores upon scores on scores of millions of "good"

Americans who must be redeemed for any gain, here, are not neighbors of your parents. You never met them. You only rile them and make their inner vices stonier, for all they see of you is your TV carnage and your hairy boys at riots, or at Woodstock Aquarian follies with their large, economy-size teeny-boppers who parade barefooted in your fiestas and join your violent pageants of vengeance.

Your assault on the university in black behalf is counter-productive in the idioglossary you both hate and don't know.

Men did reach the moon.

Racism can be made to vanish.

The first achievement was easy: the second is a trillion times harder and it will take centuries to complete, at the most optimistic estimate.

Meanwhile, you are like dreamy tots who think they can throw a penny into the sun.

For any right answer the right question must first be asked.

I have put the question.

Honkies of the world, reply!

Black people, keep the faith!

You are men, still, whatever we whiteys say.

What a pity there is no Heaven! For if there were, the Americans who got there might nearly all be black, colored or Jews.

Century after century the nonwhite peoples of the human species have suffered the ferocious oppression of white men who have called themselves Christian.

Many of these white, self-styled Christians have persecuted Jews whom these have even called a "race." They have warred with one another, also, and still do, Catholic against Protestant.

Not long ago, schoolteachers in New York, predominantly Jewish, acted as if they *were* a race, as racists, against blacks.

Now, black racism and black nationalism are presumed by many white activists among the young, and many older LIE members, to be valid counters to bet against the honkie's slashing racism . . . as if old wounds could be cured by opening new ones.

The national association of student governing bodies was recently cowed by black hoodlums to the degree that it collapsed as a parliamentary body, voted to pay "reparations" to a small and militant black outfit that cannot pretend even to represent its people, and departed in confused impotence.

No man has any choice of the color he is born.

But he does choose to be racist and Christian, though if he selects the one, the other is beyond his reach.

The white man is the fiend in this black misery.

Nothing can elevate the black man to the state he must attain for a decent existence while palefaces persist in their shame. That will come only when the honkie ceases to be the stalking demon he mostly still is.

The subject of the black American needs far deeper understanding than anybody gives it, to find, simply, a mere proper path toward resolution.

Those efforts that are being made, largely economic, in some also quite large way educative, which is a fiscal problem to a major degree, are essential but will not change the underlying cause of hate, tension, injustice and oppression.

Whitey's laws must "wither away"—as Marx put it.

Black militancy, as nationalism and racism, is the most wanton and vain way to attempt to remedy white sickness.

But, underneath all these and all allied efforts and concepts, whether good or appallingly bad, is the simple matter of our need to know what "race" is and what race means, if it does have particular meanings for particular races.

Until we understand how to improve the human breed, whether it be by prohibiting genetic defectives of all races to continue to pollute the gene pool, or by discovering some diminished capacities (and, then, for sure, some superior ones, too, in the varied races) *nothing* the racists say about other people will have any meaning at all.

I have seen many black men who had capabilities and qualities alleged to be characteristic of their kind to own which I would gladly abandon a great clutch of my "white" genetic inadequacies, if such they be. I would like to possess certain Chinese and Japanese "traits" ascribed to them as characteristic. But I am not sure, and neither is anybody else, that these admirable qualities are genetic or racial. And in fairness I might add that I, too, have a few aptitudes and traits that are not perhaps outstandingly lofty but that I think are nice and often wish were commoner among men than is the fact.

But they may be owing to my upbringing and early environs, not to the IQ, or the passionate capacities, the occasional decency or the physical endurance and strength of my forebears.

All I advocate here, then, is that we learn more about races before we undertake steps to right cosmic wrongs the blacks suffer.

The New Left, the pro-Afro activists, of course, haven't even realized these fundamental factors exist, that America's blacks cannot even move their destiny ahead a millimeter while the whitey majority remains racist in declaration or even in unconscious efforts to hide its sin by inventing a false status.

The bind is bigger than America itself.

It is older than any extant religion.

It is more terrible than any other madness of men.

And most of those young who are self-appointed solvers of the problem don't, as I said, go where the problem is, or even know the direction of the region.

13. Pot

The "drug scene" turns off all informed adults.

Any human being who has seen people with addictions of any sort knows that situation is grim.

Where "hard" drugs are involved, it is hideous.

Where amphetamines are the agent, I speak from experience. A pep pill "high" is misleading as euphoria and dangerous owing to that delusion, along with others about "elevated" capacities. It has to be paid for in equal time and equal depths of depression. And once even amphetamines become a habit, it takes more man than many men are, to shake it. A similar circumstance obtains for barbiturates. Both sorts of drugs open paths to death and injury, too, of user and the innocent public.

LSD is now known to be very dangerous.

But pot, grass, tea, marijuana is regarded as a substance different from opium derivatives and also from the high-low pills. It is not addictive though it may be habituating. It does not regularly lead to "hard" drug addiction or even to their first trial, either.

The people who have had charge of America's narcotics

enforcement laws and agencies, federal and state, have been so viciously ignorant, so vehemently and mistakenly rigid in opinion, that their malignant stupidities have largely corrupted the public and ruined the general ability to evaluate drug use.

The laws and their enforcement amount to something like a medieval holdover as repellent as witch-burning.

In the years ahead, furthermore, there will emerge hundreds or thousands of entirely new chemicals which will cause mood-shifting, mind-altering and personality-changes. They will also have other effects not now even guessed. But nobody is preparing for them, today.

Time was when any adult could buy amphetamines and barbiturates over the counter without a prescription.

Time will be, then, when these as yet unheard-of substances will probably be sold with the same carelessness.

The "drug scene," in sum, is just beginning.

But legal and medical opinion isn't even based on facts, at present. It's peculiar to read of a rock singer jailed for possession of a few pills one could have legally carried a pound of, till lately. And, certainly, the current and standing practice of classifying marijuana with heroin is literally insane.

I therefore cannot blame the grass-dosing millions of young Americans for feeling the Law, here, is vicious, and that its violation is then mandatory for free souls. No older American can justly criticize that sentiment if he violated the prohibition laws for similar "reasons" or with similar rationalizations.

Alcohol, of course, is a drug and one that ruins many times more lives than all those that require prison terms.

The "crime" resulting from drug addiction is, again, mainly not a drug-effect but a law-effect, one that makes drugs contraband, so, expensive, and forces addicts into crime merely to finance their ever-more-demanding habits.

That is a fact the lawmakers cannot weigh; and the Nixon administration has lately announced a policy of drug eradication it will rue. For it proposes to act on the circumstance least perceived by those ironheaded fools who write and who enforce law, the distinctions among drugs.

This, however, does not justify the use of marijuana or make it virtuous.

It may be, as the users insist, harmless in the sense that, however steadily used for however long a period, adverse physical effects may not ensue. The trouble with the assumption is that it is merely an assumption. The scientific knowledge of long-range result of marijuana use, of whether it shows the effect is deleterious on the average user, on specific sorts of users, or on none, is not available. But to engage in the use of a chemical (in various degrees of purity, strength, etc.) which has not been proven harmless is hardly rational.

Cigarettes, we know, are dangerous. I smoke them and have smoked them for nearly fifty years. It is stupid. I am sure I'd never have started that habit if I'd known that what we called when I was seventeen, "coffin nails," are, in fact, coffin nails.

But when a young user of pot points out that my use of tobacco and my doubts about pot amount to hypocrisy, or to a good reason for him to continue on grass, he is an equal hypocrite. For he is trying to make me live my life by his rationalizations, or vice versa. What one man does, however foolish or wrong, has no worth as alibi on what another does. Brother-keeping is invidious and doing it by a common pot-smoker's rule of "alleged lesser evil" is silly.

There is no case for pot, at all. There cannot be even if it is shown physically harmless. For even then, what case can be made for mind-blowing?

Every form of that is an escape, from heroin through pot to that mass drug, TV. Human awareness reaches its maximum intensity in the *undrugged* mind. To think it can be "heightened" by chemistry is to regard delusion and illusion as improvement. The intensification of one or of several perceptions is always made at the cost of the diminution of other faculties.

Pepped-up in seeming, or pacified, chemically, we are merely disabled.

We have become partially crippled in order to escape reality, then, not truly to widen our insights or gain inner experiences unattainable by our sober selves. I often tell myself that, if ever any drug-taker reports an inner experience I have not been able to induce cold sober, then I shall at least consider taking that route to that for me novel adventure.

What happens to these pot-users happens, actually, owing to the fact that they have no idea of the range of awareness open to their undrugged minds. The colors or sounds, visions or sensations they experience astonish them simply because they are not self-users and have only a tot-consciousness.

The drug-"expanded" mind is merely the fractional mind that hasn't learned its natural potentials, the normal potentials for sensing all things, inner and outer. But such short cuts furnish adventures which cannot be recovered when the drug wears off so that the experiment will not be of any but a dreamed value. To me, then, the pot craze is a sign of the very self-induced deprivation of which our "alienated" youth complains and not any means even to cope with that, since all the pot he can consume doesn't lessen the alienated youth's assertion of that condition.

Rather, perhaps, it increases the sense of lostness just because the "insights" he perceived under the drug cannot be recovered by him without the agent. That situation indicates how he needs to find what makes him feel alien when in a normal state: by gaining the same clues without drugs.

It can be done but the achievement isn't possible to those who seek identity by every means of self-evasion.

One other aspect of pot-use troubles me.

That one may be merely a general and psychological situation not inherent in pot smoking. The many people I knew in long-ago decades who smoked "reefers" regularly did not exhibit this phenomenon even though they used marijuana for all the years I knew them, dozens, in some instances.

But the grass-puffers of this day frequently display a different effect: a contempt of nonusers. They act like devotees of secret gods whose ritual worship sets them apart from and above the uninitiated masses. What they have said to me in person has been precisely of that quality. And many of their writings in defense of their rituals have the tone, the same implication, even when they do not make the statement in so many words.

If it is true (and I do not know it is) that pot gives such synthetic arrogance to the users, then pot ought to be outlawed absolutely and instanter. For in that case it creates an imaginary elite who assume their stoned states elevate them above normal people while, in fact, they merely intensify dreams and weaken contact with reality. There is, plainly, no basis for a presumption of superiority in any such circumstance.

It does at least somewhat exist as a species of pseudo-supremacy, now. It may not be a side effect of pot but an ego-supportive posture of contemporary pot smokers taken as a defense, actually, of a current and new doubt or guilt. Violators of prohibition, I think, also exhibited at times that kind of "superiority," though no one ever considered the man or woman who had taken three double martinis was elevated in fact—no one, that is, except the drunk, while drunk.

However, until this insidious self-sanctification of at least some pot users is proven to have no connection with the drug, the phenomenon cannot be dismissed lightly. If it proves to be a mere "positive" cover for a recently incurred sense of being or guilty, it is, still, unwarranted and dangerous to the deluded and to all others, in a way.

But if it should prove that marijuana-use produces a lingering aftereffect of deluded superiority, that would be dreadful, indeed. For, beyond any doubt, no drug provides a basis for such presumptuousness. Rather, the contrary. And if the delusion of self-importance is a side effect of the stuff, to use it is to become unbalanced utterly and dangerously, as both a social and political menace.

That possibility should be examined just as the long-term effects should be. For until we know all there is to know about marijuana, or any other drug or chemical, in their total effects on man's body, mind, well-being, health, sanity and balance, any use of them will be folly. It will be like leaping from a rock into absolute dark, unaware of whether the ground below is a foot down or a mile.

The figure is apt.

I realize, however, that all Americans, on the average, are consuming three and a half pounds, annually, of chemicals in foods, preservatives, sweeteners, shelf-life-extenders, coloring substances and so on, hundreds of chemicals about which the long-range effects are completely unknown because they are so new that no man has consumed them for long enough to provide the evidence such an assessment requires.

I realize, further, that our society is so given to doting on its "now" that it pays very little heed to the cost in its tomorrows of what it now has or now aims to get.

Smoking pot is merely one more damned fool example of an unwarranted allegation of a fictitious now-gain at a possible tomorrow-price not yet determined.

It may be far less damaging than what is in the stuff we

put in carts in supermarkets. That, still, doesn't warrant adding unknowns to those enigmas.

My point is, merely, that the gain from pot or any illegal compound is, at best, nil. The cost in time-waste at least cancels the prized delusion, dreamy visions or heightened sensibilities that are accessible swiftly, and at no money expense to the disciplined and effortful mind. Psychologically, pot is *clearly* harmful owing to the false value users place on being disoriented. A blow on the head will addle you if that's your desire.

All drugs and all medicines are, in fact, toxic to some extent. Nothing that alters body or mind chemistry does so without some harm. One not sure of the price exacted for shifting his mind about by drugs is, at the very least, one whose judgment is unreliable even for himself, let alone for others and everybody.

If anything can be called "sacred," it is man, not hemp, toadstools, speed *or* Mao-as-divine.

14. The Crisis in Identity: Episode One

Any human being who embarks on a search for his identity must begin with a single step, this one, which is a question: *Who's looking?*

For, clearly, a person who seeks self-identity cannot be without *any*. Such a one would have no way to begin, would not, by definition, even realize he needed identity.

Yet that implicit first step, it seems to me, is one the youthful seekers near-universally overlook.

Thus their identity "crisis" is in some degree owing to the fact that they fail even to know who's starting.

Answering the question correctly, on the other hand, isn't easy, and it never can be managed with complete authenticity. But the best possible knowledge of the "who" that is about to find a clearer image of that "who," is, plainly, the only way to achieve a take-off.

A person who starts seeking identity without a best-possible idea of "who he or she is, *so far*," will never even know what else to seek, or where, or how. That searcher will be trying to find more of himself, but trying as if for, somebody else, some stranger, one whose character, environment, heritage and history are unnoted, a state precluding the chase. And nobody can do anybody else's seeking. To try to do it even for a non-self is folly.

So the quest starts with a monitored self.

Who am I, to the degree I exist; and why do I, at this point, feel so poorly self-recognized that my need for further knowledge of myself is critical?

Another basic truth about identity must now be entered. Many of those in this crisis seem not to realize it is a normal "human condition" in some degree.

Nobody ever was or is ever satisfactorily self-identified.

Everybody of value is trying for added information to the end of improving his self-profile. Everybody worth a place on the planet is looking. People, and this may mean nearly all people over thirty, who are not still searching for themselves, truly are dead, walking fossils.

For inner life ends when the quest is abandoned. The "I" solidifies. It accepts itself as a finished product. All outer evidences of being alive are then mere automated responses to a psyche that has congealed.

To quests by young rebels, still another factor may be involved.

A person who opts out, cops out or drops out of the going reality, including the going system, establishment and all matters related to those, is certain to entertain intense feelings of "alienation." They are the mechanical result of such self-exile, of the fact that one has, for whatever cause, given up his identification with what exists. His reasons may seem very sound and logical, or may be very emotional and even completely specious, but the reaction, his sense of alienation is what he will have bought.

Those young people who protest their need for some new, different or added identification on the grounds that they cannot "relate" to various major aspects of the world as it is, have only themselves to pity. They tend, however, to claim angrily that the reality they have voluntarily eschewed is, itself, so false that identification with it is abhorrent. Reality is wrong, they claim. A mess. A horror. No worthy soul would want to identify with it. Ergo-reality causes my alienation.

That, of course, is a common trick of men who resent, fault or detest what's real; they put their onus on the object. It is, however, the subject who is doing the wailing.

And here is the major flaw in young rebellion.

You cannot reject reality and remain a self with any hope of identity. Granted the establishment and system, the parental values and goals, American materialism, the military-industrial self-serving structure—anything else that I have noted as wrong and all you have (that I will agree with) is just as wrong as we say, it is still *here*. It is *real*. It cannot, be escaped by psychic withdrawal, or quests in areas that do not exist.

But there is a vast difference between identifying the *reality* of all these things and identifying *with* them. In a sense, that is the thesis of this book.

The identification of the overwhelming ("silent") majority of young Americans *with* the staggering multitude of wrong, evil, trivial and fatuous attitudes, mores and activities of present adult society is, of course, a hopeless business. These people cannot be expected to do anything but perpetuate the horrors unless they change themselves.

But people who think they can banish what is, have no part of it, not even any understanding of it *as* reality, are worse off. They have no means left to deal with the real, let alone, to try to find themselves. They are in such a situation as men would be who had perceived the sinister nature of Naziism, determined to do something to change it, and then, sent shiploads of beads to Germany, or pot, or, as would be a likelier parallel here, they would be as men who undertook to wage war against Hitler's Germany without any notion of how many soldiers Hitler had, what their equipment and weapons were, what was the nature of their indoctrinated ideas, where they were, or even how to tell a storm trooper from a Dutch clergyman.

The approach to problems of the New Left, the activists, the SDS and so on, is that kind, exactly.

Don Quixote also used the method—with expectable non-results.

The matter of man's identification of himself, as a self, and man as such, is the essence of all past and present dilemmas.

The way he attempts it, and the way our young are trying to do it, is no good. It subsumes a concept of man without bothering to consider the data now at hand.

Of these data, the first is Evolution, a fact that has been known only for about a century. Almost nobody has really accepted Evolution. The post-Darwinian effort to demonstrate man was nevertheless something other than, better than, different from animals has continued as unabatedly as it went on before men knew about Evolution. Only the terms changed. Men became an "economic man" or the "thinking animal" or some other escapist invention.

So, to start seeking one's identity, to ask, "Who's searching?" is to get the first answer:

We are animals. I am an animal.

A species evolved from a primate line. Animal and nothing more. Perhaps less.

As we are animals, then, why do we see ourselves as so different from the rest?

Good question.

How *are* we different? Certainly our sense perceptions, muscular strength, size, and all other physical characteristics are surpassed in every detail and degree, by sundry other animals. Little by little the biologists have had to admit that their early criteria of "difference" were false. Some apes have opposable thumbs. Upright carriage is commonplace. Birds are bipedal. Myriads of species communicate elaborately. Chimpanzees are able to use symbols for thinking. Porpoises are capable of "original" or "creative" thought. So we come to a place where the search for a difference is confined to a mighty small area.

Most of us, however, don't get even that far. Most people (all in the LIE) are so people-fixated they have no idea how biologically crazy their orientation is. They see what people can do to objects—and even though many other species can "modify their environment"—they assume man's staggering success at that is proof enough he is no mere animal.

Man can use a whole language, speak, write, build, discover, invent, and so on—and animals can't.

But, of course, many can, a little.

What man can do better than other animals is just one thing: man can *imagine,* limitlessly, perhaps.

And that is all.

This much, and what immediately follows, I said some twenty years ago in another book.

To understand it requires a tremendous leap of the mind for the average man. He is not accustomed to looking at himself as an animal, let alone an animal that is set apart by a single increase of one animal attribute, a greater ability to imagine.

What else does man do that other animals don't do? Everybody, nearly, regresses in reply to that.

You may think at first that a city, or Einstein's theory, or your home and its furnishings, or your job, are real and not imaginary. They are real to the degree you imagine them correctly, of course. But what brought them into existence was human imagining. The ends they serve are often imaginary—and materialist to an exaggerated degree, as the kids note.

Logic and reason, you may argue, aren't imaginary but the very opposite, not dreams, but mental procedures one can prove to have reality.

Are you sure?

Ask a scientist what we know finally about reality. He will say we have no such knowledge. Ask him how firm his present knowledge is. He will say that some is very solid but much is merely a tentative image that corresponds to reality as nearly as scientists are able to manage, currently.

Ask him how real logical systems are.

He'll reply that many do correspond with reality to a degree sufficient to make them acceptable for rules about relationships and as proven means to learn more nearly correct concepts of additional reality. But he will point out that all logical systems are imaginary constructs and only those which have been found to have permanent validity are even tentatively acceptable. Many other logics are pure abstractions, imaginary systems that often do not seem to relate to anything real that's known. Still other systems are logical for one purpose but cannot serve for another. We have no unified field theory. And no idea of what logics must still be invented to relate those we imagine suitable now, let alone to give accurate images of realities we as yet don't even imagine to exist, that may prove to be real and so, become logically imaginable.

Imagination, I said long ago, is the ability to "enter time" by the use of images, or symbols for them, and by logical inventions of all sorts—proven, speculative, irrelevant or actually known to be undemonstrable.

Man, for more than other animals, can remember the past and what he learned in it from others or by experience. That memory is wholly imagined since its source is past, gone, not at hand, vanished, destroyed, and only as "real" as the retained image in its correspondence. But we can imagine the past in the present. And we can make permutations and combinations of all that imagined past, that memory, for purposes in our future.

The future is not here either, and so, we merely imagine it, too, when we act or plan now for ends in a time we only imagine.

Except for being able to remember, to create images of the past in the mind, and for being able to use a similar process about the future, our present, our now, is the only reality and the present is, itself, "real" only as our senses perceive it.

Our running "now" is therefore real only as is the time sense and awareness of other animals. And the demand for "now-gratification" of youth is like—and unlike—animal demand. It is hedonistic when it is enjoyed; painful, when what is happening right now hurts.

So our identity at any present moment will be in fact as real only as that of any other animal. All we can add to it will be imaginary and composed of images from the past or of the future and not one of them *will be real*, at all! These images will not even be correct unless they are correctly imagined—correctly recalled and/or correctly foreseen.

But what are we *doing*, in a present defined here as a state that can be only sense-perceived, since past and future images are also involved in our present?

We are simply entering time by imagination.

But we do not do that by accurate images, necessarily. We often make images that don't match past facts or do not furnish correct future concepts.

I gave the following speculative example of wrong use of imagination in that old book:

Man's ability to enter and "use" time by imagination enabled him to conceive, ages ago, of a truth that animals with lesser powers of image-making had not perceived.

All living creatures die.

Man dies.

But as the image of that truth crept into some at-first-murky human minds, it must have caused a shock. There was nothing like the experience in all those billion-plus years of ancestral creatures.

All other animals were (and all are) largely "existentialists." In their natural states they see the fact of death and the death of their own kind. But their behavior shows they do not and cannot connect that circumstance with their own selves and future.

What the discoverers of death found was that region in time's dimension where each and every man would vanish. The result was that the prior state of now-being had to include the new fact of not-being. The pioneers had entered the dimension by imagination of time and could not deny that death lay there.

But they evidently were self-identified as "man" even at that time. The elaboration of consciousness which enables our species to "use time," as I've put it, had by then doubtless permitted those ancients to develop skills and pass them on, to communicate with a rude language and to perform other acts which led them to regard their breed as different and superior. The argument for that is found in what they soon did about the new and dreadful knowledge of mortality.

The faculty that had led to the discovery was made to serve for evasion of the seemingly intolerable and surely biologically unprecedented finding. They imagined they had a spirit, soul or shade that did not perish with the body. And that was not difficult because the attribute which seemed to support their conviction of superiority, the ability to imagine, seemed and was, in fact, invisible, mysterious, immaterial.

Behind those men was the pressure of all evolution that had created only an existential awareness, a consciousness of the moment, or a near moment. Man's ancestral forms felt fear when deadly perils were at hand, injuries, illnesses or onslaught by predators. But even in such present-time situations they did not foresee death. They had not previously recognized the sure fate, in any present, so they could not see it in a present period, however lethal.

When man was forced to live in all his present with the knowledge of death, his frenzied wish to escape from that very costly "price" of his lone advance led him to invent a soul that was immortal, an artifact derived from the invisible entity he already somewhat knew as a serf.

For a long time man invested all beings and even objects and the forces of nature with parallel souls. But as his use of imagination for material ends became more sophisticated he was obliged to invent concepts of immortality that seemed less naive. He has done that ever since, maybe for hundreds of thousands of years and certainly for tens of thousands.

If the invention of an afterlife were honestly derived and true as a result, men would, of course, have eventually developed one, single "religion" with appropriate right-wrong systems for its expression in living. Since, however, one finds in any minor American town a dozen temples raised for the worship of diverse figures of God and eternal life, it is manifest that from our first exploitation of the mind to escape the knowledge of mortality, no validity exists in *any* such convictions and beliefs. They are sustained as true by an *abuse* of the imagination called faith which is useless for establishing any truth.

Readers with "modern" ideas may find the foregoing con-

cept as both obvious and unnecessary owing to the fact they
have given up all religious notions and acknowledged that
their death will be total and final. But have they given up
the corollaries? Other faith-founded fictions?

So far as I am aware, my presentation of the theoretical
etiology of religion was the first of its sort. Once seen it is
rather self-evident. And in the near quarter century since the
idea was published many scholars have employed to it, as if
it had always been an item in their scientific baggage and,
surely, not one put there by a layman. But they usually fail,
as the reader may have failed, to see certain broader implications of the idea.

Archaeology shows how far back in time man had invented
many variations of his immortality myth. But archaeologists,
like anthropologists and, for that matter, tourists in alien
lands, devote themselves to the notice of differences. So, of
course, do those lowliest of scientists, taxonomists. Taxonomists, however, though they engage in listing minutiae of di-
versities, also do see broader relationships and enter races
into species and these into genera. The others don't, much.
So we, as contemporary men, however we may imagine ourselves scientific, find the *diversity* of peoples, their social customs and cultures of exclusive interest. We rarely note their
identities, that all are parallel and serve the identical end of
human survival, by whatever means are locally regarded as
most efficient and also, as "moral."

Perhaps this near-universal regard of others as different is
an unconscious means of maintaining the illusion they, too,
sustain, in their special, cultural ways. This is the illusion
of human separateness from the rest of living beings and
there, of local superiority by the separateness, by differences
that are, all, superficial.

We are all born of women from eggs fertilized by males.
We are fed and raised and taught the local speech, methods

and myths. We grow up to plant, collect, hunt or slaughter food. We suffer pain from the same causes and rejoice over identical or parallel events and achievements. We mate and reproduce, grow old and die. We are then expected, by nearly all contemporary people, still, to enter one or another form of afterlife.

These processes are common to all mankind and the variations of their styles are trivial. But until that is realized we will not be able to perceive our simple identity as a species, or that we are all animals, as well. Darwin's findings will not have been assimilated till then. The search for individual identity will therefore continue to be mistaken, truncated, even impossible as a solid feat.

For what has been surmised here about early man's perception of death and his subsequent invention of immortality of his "soul," represents an early and an enormous misuse of imagination, perhaps his first corruption of his attempt to gain a human identity. Magic thinking, as Freud called it, acted there. And the most objective, atheistic, science-oriented and truth-seeking person of this day will, with very few exceptions, proceed from flaws like that one which occurred in an ancient perversion of mind. He will believe his "thinking" does, indeed, represent his separation from the primate and earlier ancestral forms to some new class and category that makes him distinct and altogether superior.

Few of us accept that we are only animals and wholly animals. Few, in fact, know enough about what animals are to entertain that mere thought with calm. And young people, striving for their identities in the current "crisis," won't likely have had time enough, or access to a sufficient amount of the relevant materials, let alone, the necessary experiences, even to begin the corrective steps needed for true self-knowledge.

The discovery of death was man's first major identity-crisis.

He failed to face it, for very simple motives of which none was honest.

With that sad calamity as his start he made a second dismal flub on meeting his next crisis in this vital affair.

15. The Crisis in Identity: Episode Two

That man is only now trying to correct his gross misidentification of himself in relation to nature is a tragedy and may cause man's last tragedy. The impending calamities owing to his error here may already be past reversal. Even if we are not in a doomed situation we certainly soon shall be unless enough of us alter current attitudes, values and convictions in degrees for which no precedent exists. At present, not one person in ten thousand, even of those who are aware of man's sabotage of the biosphere, of his ecological follies and the general danger from them, is also aware enough of their complexity and numbers to do any useful thinking in behalf of human survival and continuity.

Even professional ecologists are not usually knowledgeable enough in areas outside the sciences (of which *all* are involved in ecology) to make reasonable guesses about what has to be done, if possible, to keep the planet habitable. The research hasn't started. Those who could do it fail to understand the resistance that such effective efforts would encounter, the fantastic cost that the task makes mandatory or even how to communicate what they do know to the public.

Laymen are so much worse off that it is hard to see how they can be shown that preliminary fact. Everybody is "against" pollution. No one is for it and there seem to be no neutrals, either. And the new legions of instant-ecologists imagine that palpable pollution is the whole of our environmental troubles. Besides, the negative approach (which is the current and growing kick of the students and the under-thirties) tends to disorient people who might, otherwise, become more properly aligned.

The student anti-pollutionists are by now near-pros at opposition. But their opposition to pollution is characteristic of the bulk of their past means of protest. One of them recently put it neatly. "Who needs more studies of pollution?" he asked. "You can see it, smell it and touch it." The observation was prompted by an official reaction to anti-pollutionists stating that more research was a prior condition to action. This was called a cop-out.

The inference of that example can be widened. Student rebels do not want to do any studying whatever in the sciences—that one area which must be employed and extended to furnish a hope that man can save the world for people. Science and technology, as I must note again and again, is at the top of the rebel students' list of "irrelevant" subjects.

These youths are anti-science and anti-technology for the same "reason" they are opposed to so much else. Science and technology are, to them, a basic causal agent in the culture they loathe, ergo, they reject them and refuse to learn their content.

Here, the only suitable if minute approach has been taken by a few but it is at least positive: the demand, as a *right* of everyone, for a clean and perpetually livable environment. Even so, the only agent of our fearful ecological situation is not yet perceived by the individual as *himself*.

The quality of any environment is a function of the quality

of people. Included in that theorem are all those who inhabit any particular environ.

That idea will be hard to teach.

For we still believe almost unanimously in the ancient and universal error about man's identification in relation to nature.

That blunder was forgivable so long as man had not yet endeavored to observe cause and effect honestly. But when he did begin to do so, he might have had a chance to use that tool, fresh-forged in his imagination, for more ends than was the fact. His uses were largely limited to cause-and-effect studies (and conclusions therefrom) which provided material advantages and status-giving items, in man's fancy, or, what we call progress.

Possibly his ongoing beliefs about his superiority owing to his invented immortality and the associated fabrications prevented wider uses of the new tool, that of logic, honesty, reason and inductive reasoning. Certainly, the rare men who tried to state a logically-reached truth that was antithetical to current mythologies were usually hung, poisoned, burned alive or tortured to death for their "heretical" or "atheistic" suggestions.

Probably, man failed there because he had long since achieved so great and so corrupt a sense of his eminence, his divinity, his ownership of the earth and all life forms (all of which no one and no group ever can own but only has the use of), that his ideas were of nature as inferior, although something to fear, fight and manage if possible, but always to know as at once lesser and the enemy. The way he saw the evidence, supported that view for ages, since he used sight and mind (he called both) to support his arrogant self-image, established in the initial crisis of identity and man's ensuing failure to meet it honestly.

The position that nature was antagonistic to man but that

man stood above it was very odd, though it remains our almost unanimous stance.

Until very recent times men took it to be an unassailable truth, however clearly a paradox. The elements devastated man. Diseases and plagues struck him down out of nowhere. The wilderness, forest, swamp, open seas, lakes, rivers, desert, mountains, were dangerous, forbidding and full of unexpected hazards to all who adventured into or upon them. Wild beasts tore men apart. Some things, animal and vegetable and mineral, too, that he ate, killed him. Some of these did so at certain times and not at others. Nature was hostile, hateful and not even predictable.

But as eons passed, this animal was making headway at what finally became a very rapid and amazing pace. He learned to grow food and domesticate animals to eat and to do his work and to transport himself. He learned to build houses and temples and soon, cities. He slowly learned, by trial and *success* (Lorenz' correction of the behaviorist's blunder) how to mitigate his risks. Sometimes, by using past memory in his present for future dreaming and figuring, he hit on quite basic laws and logics, such as mechanical principles and techniques for exploiting natural forces to his advantage.

He even learned how to make symbols for his spoken words, how to write.

In these millennia, he often discovered correct and great images of reality and then soon mislaid them, lost them. Sometimes his wars destroyed the record. Sometimes his new religions swept the true ideas and genuine facts away as abominations. Eratosthenes knew the earth was a globe and measured it to within fifty miles of radius; but nearly two thousand years would pass before the idea was found anew, and, for most of that time, the Christian world had rejected it on pain of death. In the country of the blind the one-eyed man is *killed*.

By the time the pyramids were rising in Egypt, and maybe tens of thousands of years before then, the animal that is man had lied about that self-awarded state in every way he could invent and serviced it by any means to keep the faith and silence those who had a better idea.

To Christianity, man's supremacy was fundamental. The earth was his property and all life was subject to his ordinance as the servant of God. And by then, of course, his actual situation, as one species of animal whose very existence was dependent on intricate relationships of millions of other species, wasn't even imaginable. The imaginary God had addled everybody.

Any number of "highly educated" people today keep saying that we have now actually conquered nature, or nearly, or that we have controlled nature, or will do it soon.

To such people, the old image of man not only holds but is seemingly reinforced by our scientific and technical achievements. Even when they acknowledge those attainments are being sustained at some cost in environmental pollution, they still imagine technological man has conquered nature, or will, and also that he should and must. Eliminating the present, adverse effects of this "conquest" is seen by such people as merely the problem of extending nature-conquest.

Of course, that's *all* imaginary.

And all *untrue*.

The laws of nature are sufficiently known to make any such posture indecently vain. They are inexorable laws. No resource is inexhaustible. Every violation of a law of nature committed by any step of so-called progress will demand ultimate redress.

Man can exist only within the laws and tolerances of nature. Those who believe in God, in any supreme being, cannot, alas, think at all. Their faith, their superstitious use of their brains, guarantees the output will be false.

It may still seem hard for the reader to imagine all the "inner" and "mental" processes for which philosophers, psychologists and many other kinds of learned men have given so many names, as, simple, the varied workings of imagination.

Through the ages men have resisted that too-simple-seeming truth. To accept it, means (they imagine) that they must then accept their own theories, dreams, definitions, reason, logic, feeling, evaluating, intuition, ideas, education, beliefs as imaginary. *Of course!* But the crucial fact, there, is the *accuracy* of their imagining, if any.

All we can do is imagine.

Even in our "now," and any "here," what we may regard as reality that our senses "perceive" is not, as everybody knows, all that is "real" in the present and our presence. There may be sounds we cannot hear. We don't see microscopic life that we know abounds. Great surges of electromagnetic waves are crashing through and around us which we can only make "real" by turning on our radio, TV, or some other instrument. A direct, present-time experience with matter and energy is limited by our senses which do not inform us of innumerable and powerful phenomena that are equally real. Even to try to add such *unsensed* realities requires . . . *what?* Imagination, plainly: a use of images from past learning to envisage what is known to be part of the scene but known only as once learned and now, but image.

Further, in this now-partly-real-and-partly-sensed situation, our information, including that which is directly received from our surroundings or which describes our bodily states, will be altered by imagination. We will be involved in present perceptions in some personal manner that will be imaginary in that it will not proceed from the things around us but from some past-formed response within us or future-guessed to them.

If you are in a room, for instance, it can be one you chose and furnished to your taste; and so, it may give you a sense of satisfaction, snugness, of a crystallized expression of yourself, offering comfort and other positive things that are pleasant but that are pleasant because you imagined the scene and then arranged it for that private and unique purpose. But maybe you will dislike a certain chair. You may note the room needs sweeping. There may be a kitchen odor in it that you dislike.

What are you *doing* where you are, then? How long will you be *content* with that? And when your contentment diminishes, or the time to do something else arrives, you will leave the room, or change what you are doing. If you didn't, imagine your rising discomfort! But none of those matters would relate to the room. All such would concern your image of yourself, both as of now, and then, as of later, in the not-arrived future.

The reason people have so much difficulty in accepting this act of image-making in past and future time, as the *only* extra thing we "do" in our heads, is owing to the fact it is further hidden by false premises about "reality." We consider so much of what exists as real and, in fact, we do so widely imagine it correctly, that we don't feel any need to distinguish between the many correct images and the many that are mistaken, let alone those we accept and cherish that are purely inventions and have no proof.

So, self-identity next involves an examination (by imagination used correctly) of our *value-systems*.

Everybody has a value-system. It is necessary merely to exist. One must have a general sense of what's right and what's wrong or one would soon make fatal mistakes. A great deal of the early training of infants concerns such basic right-wrong values. And this instruction goes on through childhood. It should continue through life but it usually does not. Somewhere along the way, most of us settle for rigid values-systems of countless, conflicting kinds.

A baby should (or shouldn't) suck its thumb. A baby shouldn't (we say) fondle its genitals for pleasure. A boy should find the ball he lost because it cost money. But he should not run across the street to do that, until he is sure there is no oncoming car. And on, on, on, forever, it seems.

The next step, then, is to ask: What is *my* value system? What does this self, that is searching for more of itself, currently regard as the greatest good, the worst evil? What subsidiary standards have I?

Here, ethologists, scientists who study animal behavior, have given us a new yardstick. One of the startling observations they've made is startling only because it has been perfectly visible to man, in all his ages, but only recently noted in its true way.

Every individual in every species of animal, with one exception, follows a right-wrong program that has a single result: the provision of the best possible conditions for that creature's next generation.

So, from a viewpoint not human, but one that considers all animals from what would be *their* "viewpoint," if they could imagine one, every species is completely *moral!* Two-sexed or asexual, each being lives in a way that causes it to do the right acts, and to avoid the wrong ones, which in the end supply the ideal behavior for the ongoing life of its species.

Men have so prejudiced this scene with their own, mistaken images of right and wrong that most of them even now can't see that universal truth about the goal of "lower" beings and their "moral" rules for that. Men have been revolted by so many processes that are right for other species, or frightened by them, or annoyed, that they haven't even tried much to ask whether or not acts that have a negative effect on them are—or aren't—right for the offending animal.

They see nature as red in claw and fang, bloody, predatory, hateful, malevolent and wild. Only lately have a few begun to see that the lioness' leap on the weakest or sickest or a crippled member of a zebra herd isn't "violence," or "aggression," but the lion's way of doing what we call "shopping" and "eating."

They see a cow tormented by a parasite and never notice that the parasite also is just eating, in its way.

Certainly, people don't relate the sight of a big beast being eaten alive by larvae to their *own* ways. It never occurs to them that *man* is a *parasite* on *everything*, living or inert! What man cannot use or consume, he carts to dumps or destroys if it's alive, *because* it's in *his* way. Owing to his effort to plant a crop or havest one, to quarry something he can use or consume, or mine it, he is a parasite on what he wants and also on what's in his way.

He resists that greedy image because he has not yet accepted the fact that he, too, is an animal. He is far from wondering if his right-wrong value-system should be revised for the goal of all other animals.

Even if he does see that all other living beings are "moral" for each species, and even if he sees the next truth, that all species living in any one area are subject to more general laws, he will not easily see that man has ignored that otherwise universal system for each species and for their communities.

For example, wolves prey on caribou. But the caribou the wolves pull down for food will be the weakest in a herd, the sick, the very old, the unguarded young, not the strongest, brightest and most healthful members. So wolves are unconscious feeders of champion caribou. Their shopping for supper assures the herd of the survival of the best stock by culling out the inferior or defective animals.

That is but one, simple example of tens of millions of similar interrelationships of living beings, predators and their prey, included. Yet "wolf" is our common symbol for the supposed ferocity of wildlife! There is no record anywhere I can find of a wolf or wolves making an attack on a person. Wolves just won't harm people in the wilds and if you didn't know that, you have a chance to guess how far you are from any ability to make sense about the animal *you* are.

It is man who is the wild animal. He has rejected that value-system which the rest of earth's creatures follow for survival. Of course, they don't know the purpose of their behavior, or why doing this and this is right and doing that would be wrong, for them, wrong because it would diminish that creature's final end of providing the best possible chance for its offspring, or, right because, in one way or another and however, indirectly, a right act serves that result.

Men, of course, give some attention and value to their next generations. As father-mother, their own kids may be the only beneficiaries, or maybe the kids of friends or American kids. Whatever they contribute will include their religious beliefs, traditions, culture, political ideology and all else they think posterity should be given.

Human "morals" therefore do not really exist.

They are not even based on the one moral system by which men must be guided if they are ever to know what is truly right or wrong for people. Other breeds pursue an end they do not and cannot limit, brainwash or even know.

The disassociation of contemporary youth from nature is

greater than that of any people in all time. It is so vast, so absolute, so near universal in the young that their chance of sane self-identification as animal is very slight. They are *urban*. Their reference-points are exclusively "human" and concern politics, economics, sociology, psychology and other homocentric topics of the LIE. When they speak accusingly of "pollution" and of a "degraded environment" they blame their elders and their industries for what they imagine to be stupid but remediable circumstances. To them, what's wrong with the environment is only what threatens people. The treat to the galaxies of life-systems sustaining man is unintelligible. They know nothing of nature beyond paved roads and city parks.

What urban person, for example, even muses on the source of his dinner? What city-dweller bothers to distinguish its elements in terms of their origins? How many pounds of what does it take to put a serving of beef or lamb or pork on his plate? How many trees had to be cut down and how much nitrogen fixed, what phosphates and fuel are needed to provide his vegetables, the apples in his pie, or his paper napkin?

Some urbanites, even some who imagine they are bright, like the late George Bernard Shaw, learn a bit and are so revolted by man's eating of meat that they associate flesh-eating with the common view of "predation" by other animals. These fools become "vegetarians" as if to become saintlier by avoiding the "savagery and aggression" most people attribute to animals, that is not true of any animal *but* man.

How vicious are the millions who hunt creatures as a "noble sport!" What pleasures they take in the craft of the gunsmith and their skill as marksmen! How gleefully they grade their fun! The bigger the quarry, the rarer, the more remote its habitat and the more "dangerous" the beast—the more glorious the kill! Let them think of what *should*, by their own rules for "fun," be the most sport possible: an open season on *man*. Here is a big animal and the most cunning as well as the deadliest. In an open season on man, hunters might even realize that what is sport for them is not so amusing or thrilling to "game." Hunters of non-men are lower than predators for hunters prey on the best breeding stock.

Most of us never see the wilderness. We are reluctant to stop at the side of a pasture bordering a freeway where the unfamiliar weeds and trees have a disquieting effect. Grazing cattle nearby supply milk and cream and butter and beef, as they may realize, but they are anxious about these creatures pastured beside the throughway and not interested until they appear as steaks on their tables or cream in a pitcher. They ought to visit a slaughterhouse to understand a little better what man is, and needs, and how he satisfies such needs.

Our dependence on the chain of life is absolute. Not to understand that is to understand nothing about humanity. It is to be "identified" exclusively with man's images of himself and accompanying cultural results as all the value there is and all man needs to cherish to continue his cultural rise. That is not an identity but the sure way for men to perish altogether.

So, when the activists bellow that America is sick or poisoned, they merely bellow. The *world* is *insane*—and in a far more horrible way than they can imagine. The sickness *they* decry is not even a major symptom of the underlying ill, that they are as riddled with as their opponents. They are ridiculous. Their aims are absurd. And those young who intend to enter the establishment as it exists and help operate the present system, expanding it too, are equally victims of the ageless epidemic.

The proper means toward cure is seen by men who have

not yet made it evident to more than one other man in ten thousand, even in America. And when the enlightened one tries to explain the proper therapy, his audience will perhaps even nod, understand a little, briefly, and walk out to continue spreading the disease in more virulent forms —efforts to increase production, to demand more goods for all people and to "politicize" others for that aim—forgetting swiftly that the politics of nature is the only dialectic.

What some young people see as a social crisis, then, is only a trivial incident, one hardly pertinent to the crisis of technological men who do not realize the cause of what they have brought upon themselves, now, and will suffer in the near future.

The very idea that political, racial and economic "solutions" are proper ones is morally unworthy and intellectually off course. People who make such causes their whole concern are people who could not, in a lifetime, find one other bug, snake or barnacle that stupid, that unethical.

16. The Crisis in Identity: Episode Three

Until recent times a popular way to evade acknowledging ourselves as animals was to say we were "moral animals." Human behavior in the past fifty years has somewhat drowned the plausible sound of that gimmick.

We are *able* to be *ethical*. The discipline of science rests in that fact. The scientist's endeavors will be undertaken and performed with the utmost honesty. When a scientist cheats he is no longer qualified as such. And when any other human being does, his victim is also himself.

The very widespread and fairly new practice of cheating by students has bemused me, for it indicates such crooks have not yet caught on to what study and learning mean. Tedious rationalizations are offered: that the pressure to pass compelled cheating, that the worthlessness of the course made cheating the only good means of saving time, or, and this especially, that the *adult* world is populated by cheats.

The only cause for cheating is cowardice. No cheat ever had the courage of the dumbest student who would not do so low and self-mutilating a deed for any cause. And to cheat because older people cheat, as a sort of revenge and alibi, is a craven reaction. But most of the young revolutionaries operate that way. To whatever they deplore they react by supporting the envisaged opposite, or, as here, by the presumption that perfidy by other justifies one's own. Such responses are void of personal identity. Man *can* have ethics even morals now though morals are largely beyond him, still. And when students excuse their cheatfulness by pointing to cheatful elders in the establishment, aren't they *joining it* at the lowest level, too?

If man were moral in the only possible way, that of all other animals, he'd also have a single value-system fitted to his species.

Any different code destroys the species and so its meaning. Any basic right-wrong doctrine that is different from the universal will automatically deny future men that vital chance which they will have only if their good is everybody's ruling concern. Where that is not the case, the result will always be that man's meaning, to him, is found wholly in his *current condition*. All say that man means as much as he ever will, here and now.

To imagine our current and countless right-wrong creeds are valid and will be for posterity is to imagine man has all the knowledge, insight and excellence he can ever gain. It is to act as if the assorted code holders were really God, and had made the laws of nature, too. And that generations to follow would not need other ideas or find any. Such moralists don't even note the immense and varied competing systems. *But why?*

A person who believes in an afterlife, to illustrate the answer, will, of course, have a right-wrong rule book for attaining that imagined state in eternal bliss, or peace, and the rule book will likely show, too, what hellish penalties must be paid eternally for violations of the ordinances. Merely in trying to do what is good and to avoid doing evil for that wholly selfish end of a false hope about happy eternity, a man or woman will devote great amounts of time and energy to some random kind of rule-following, temple-attendance, churchgoing, prayers, an infinitely elaborate dictionary of huggermugger with costumes, rites and trinkets that are holy and symbolic—and God-ordained participation in those magic labors will have no relation to the ongoing of the species, the only "immortality" that is even theoretically real. These people will be stealing that much time and energy, interest and attention from their very own children, and all men to be, to stock up for their own, totally self-centered and completely imaginary reward in their corpse state.

An identity of that sort, though the commonest, is not moral in any way. It is perfect vice. It diminishes the opportunity of future men-to-be to mean more than those vain believers allow. Belief in an afterlife and in the propagation of whatever its rules may be is a more evil act against all other men than war, any war, all war, even Atilla's brand.

The ethologists have given us, recently, some further insights into animal behavior that seem very useful in this criminal matter.

Many species of animals are "territorial."

Territorial mammals exhibit two forms of aggression. A group of any such species will occupy an area the size of which is defined by the space-need of individual numbers of that species and that group. When other groups of the same species threaten to encroach on such a territory, its occupants will defend its boundaries aggressively. Inside each group's borders there will be a second aggressive struggle, for status, the conflicts that set up "pecking orders."

This sounds and seems so much like human behavior that it has been used as a description of the nature of man's massive aggression as innate and as expressed to defend this territory, his nation, and also, in the second way, to

achieve status on his group-turf. Robert Ardrey put forward
that idea, for one.

But what is true of territorial animal aggression that isn't
true of the human form? Convincing people that aggression
is part of the human package, like a stomach, is as popular
as redeeming them from original sin and about the same:
an excuse to be bastardly.

*In all territorial species other than man, aggression is
ritualized. The border scrap is broken off before anybody is
really hurt. The pecking-order battles stop short of fatality,
when one of the contestants either moves away or gives some
signal the opponent recognizes as surrender.*

That aspect of animal aggression, used to hold territory,
or to gain status within a territory, but always by means
short of slaughter, does not even approach man's aggression.
Death in territorial or status conflicts among other lifeforms,
when it happens, is rare and owing to accident. Even man
tries to limit fatal consequences of *status*-conflict by en-
forcing the laws of tribes or nations. But when man engages in warfare against another group of his species dwelling outside his territory, or even a hostile group within, he
is a mass killer whose murderousness has no parallel in
nature. *His* ritual there is to kill to the limit, not to stop
short of murder.

Why?

Some years ago in *The Magic Animal* I put forward a
theory to explain man's absolute and terrible departure from
the otherwise binding limits of territorial animal aggression.

I think my idea may help any person willing and able
to ponder it, in a quest for personal identity.

It concerns my other theory about that other difference I see between man and other species, man's imagination, and his use of that for all inner process except present-
time sensory perceptions.

The thought is very simple.

It is simply the suggestion that man identifies himself with what he "knows" and what he "believes" to be "true." His individual knowledge and belief, then, are "territories" of his imagination and he identifies with those "holdings," whether they are correctly imagined or not, theological, scientific, hearsay, whatever.

Where those holdings are not correctly imagined, or even where they are not demonstrable by such means as can show other truths to be that, the owner of the images is in trouble. For if that region of his inner (imaginary) belief is attacked, or even criticized, he cannot, obviously, defend it as everybody can defend correctly-envisioned concepts.

No *rational* defense of imagined but unprovable territory is possible obviously. Further, no rational means are available to my sample man for the propagation, promotion or transmission to others of his incorrectly envisaged—or unprovable—territory. But since he identifies his "I" with such subjective holdings, he has either to assume them right and true or alternatively, change *himself*. But all these convinced territorial imagists will tend to regard change of belief as comparable to a mutilation of the body. A fundamentalist Christian, say, would feel that becoming a self-identified and open atheist, or a Moslem, would amount to the ruin of his inner identity and be as bad as or worse than having his eyes gouged out or his legs cut off.

On that account, any real or seeming threat by others to his "inner territory," or any contrary or debunking idea others offer, will appear to be a menace of a very deadly sort. Without rational support, there being none for these people, how can they respond to such apparently destructive "aggressions?" The owner of mistaken or unprovable grounds, will have nothing left as defense save *irrational* acts. He will therefore meet all presumed threats to his "territory" in senseless ways. Even those which would be enlightening and *improve* his concepts while adding to his self-identity, seem equivalents of physical assault! He reacts and reacts out of a real emotion risen in his unreal self-view.

His irrational behavior will be of limitless violence when such assumed assault is seen as a magnitude requiring any and every measure of counter-aggression for the maintenance of what we have defined as either incorrect belief or belief that cannot be rationally proven.

To behold man as a being whose self, whose identity, whose "I" is defined by whatever subjective territory he regards as true, to see all of that, in all men, as imaginary, is to behold a biological paradigm for man's hideous, constant and deadly aggression.

The real world is, to each of us, what we imagine it to be. It cannot be other. What a man *is*, to him, is whatever he happens to hold true, whether by learning, reason or by "faith."

Of course, some men try to extend and modify that inner territory so as to imagine reality with ever-improved accuracy. That is what education should undertake to do for all. Science attempts to provide ever-clearer descriptions and ever-more precise boundaries of images of reality by investigating them with logical methods, honestly, and open-mindedly, in order that better results of fresh survey may be used to revise the scientist's inner territorial holdings. What men believe that is not susceptible of rational examination, science will or should disregard.

And, of course, science has very swiftly used its special morality, its "honesty applied to objects" and its logical systems that were invented and then tested and shown correct for at least certain procedures, to provide an improved image of the universe, of nature and man, himself. That present image is complex, vast in proven survey and rich in territories that *are* correctly imagined. The same contributions of science have shown that the kingdoms of conviction with which most people identify are not only fictitious and not tenable by men of knowledge and reason, but how these dreamed badlands were invented, and why.

It is asking much of any living individual to ask that he examine his current inner world by comparing it with what science has found true, just to see where his own passionately held, present territory may be mistaken dogma, no longer defensible.

But modern man, honestly seeking his identity, will *have* to do that to own a self that is as nearly real as present knowledge makes possible.

Not to do that is to remain a victim of one's own mistaken inner territory, a needless cripple, a maniac, an owner of hand-me-downs.

And that is who we mostly are, animals crippled or mad by our own misused imagination: people who try to convert all others to their territorial images as a righteous act, when it is reasonless aggression; people who defend territories that are imagined, that don't exist, that are corruptly seen, with the one means left to them—aggression, and without any limit, when they feel a pressure of reason requires such self-defense.

The LIE, the New Left, take note. That territory is not just unreal and in error, but see how you try to *defend* it!

How is our inner realm established? What are our pious "grounds" of belief? How are the areas of knowledge that scientists even call "fields" surveyed? Why are some areas held by us with all violence to keep them unchanged, or, as with scientists, kept open and hospitable to change, including abandonment, if need be?

The answers are not many or very abstruse.

What we are taught as children by our parents and what

we infer, too, that they do not mean to reveal, is part of our domain. The culture contributes a very great part. Education adds more and of that some of its contribution comes from outside a given culture. But we are presented with much unexamined tradition. A religion is handed us as the main field and that is done usually before most people are old enough to doubt anything in such areas. We extend our inner real estate by reading, by looking at TV and by accepting what people say. The input is massive but we arrange it, whether conscious that we are doing that or not, according to our individual sense of vital values, our sense of what comprises truth or nontruth, right or wrong, good or evil, moral or amoral, and of what is useful to ourselves or not—and there, irrespective of any doubt of the judge or the evidence. We *are* the judges.

Who will have given the values we so use? Why do we believe what we were led to call our realm and self?

We accept authority, our taught or self-crowned judgment of authority, even Mao's! We accept, too, in some large degree, fields of information and of laws and rules that have been scientifically found, tested and proven, unless these mar our master map. And we accept a great area of belief on faith. Faith is, in fact, the trick we use to kid ourselves into accepting a great part of our inner realm. That is, then, nonprovable and the trigger of murder-as-"defense."

It is a bizarre method for a being with ample imagination to do better. And one of the most powerful demonstrations of our animal state is just this use of faith instead of reason. Animals other than ourselves cannot reason much and their evaluations have to be made as if on "faith," from innate guides, instincts, a little learning only, but animals have far too little imagination to cheat themselves, their breed and nature.

With the animal, man, there is a tendency to act from what, in other animals, supplies drives that require no conscious appraisal. Man believes alone, and acts because he has *faith* in teachings and sources, and their authorities as man-determined. These can be any sort, any person or any creed: the Pope or Billy Graham, Marx and Engels, the John Birch Society, the Bible or Mrs. Eddy. But all such accepted territory will be appropriated by faith and held above demonstrable faulting, reasonable criticism or rational examination.

Faith, in short, is the use of and reliance on our capacity for mindless soaking up of beliefs by suggestion and autosuggestion. It is our willingness to arrive at what we will then call truth, *by cheating*, that blows man's mind. By *faith*. Faith is that inner operation by which the mind agrees it will accept as absolute truth an image or many images which will be seen as true and absolute only *after* the prior agreement is made to "take the material on faith."

Belief in God depends on the prior act of agreeing one will believe in God. Following the agreement, then, one does.

Much of what all of us, or nearly all of us, accept as true, is established by using versions of that mechanism—and it's established, then, beyond the reach of logic, because we have promised beforehand to assume we are so right we need not even submit what we "know by faith as truth," to inspection. We'd "rather die"—and much rather *kill!* The task of trying to undo such self-deceits is not widely attempted. Even science was not permitted to examine human beliefs achieved through faith until recently. Faith made closed areas. Darwin himself agonized over the fact that his dawning perception of evolution was antireligious. And Marxists are precisely as unwilling to allow their secular religion to be subjected to scrutiny.

Faith, then, is surely the most corrupt use man can make of his capacities for imagining since they include potentials for imagining with reason, in the new-born, at least.

This leads to a next question:

What is truth? No search for identity can be attempted without a means for answering *that* one!

I have already said that truth is any image of reality that corresponds to the object, process or phenomenon. I've said, too, that at least very broadly usable truth resides in those invented logical systems which have been tested and affirmed as proper routes to confirming our images as real, finding more images of reality, to making those we have more nearly correct and to seeking other images of the real that will be new and yet true as far as old or some new but tested logic then confirms.

But, simply owing to the fact that men are still bogged down in disputes over truth, I have, too, studied that debate and reached a conclusion, or a theory, which seems to offer a new way to evaluate whatever is said to be true.

In a personal communication from Dr. Konrad Lorenz he asked the question and added that some things, surely, were true beyond question. As I've noted elsewhere, he illustrated with the truth that the earth revolves around the sun. There must be, he implied, a vast category of such indisputable truths. But the problem is how to select or evaluate them, was his further inference.

Thinking of that, I realized that the dimension of time, the one men enter by imagination, is useful as a method for classifying "truth."

How could one find that area of undeniable truth Konrad postulated?

It consists of those images of reality which represent phenomena and processes that are not time-related. The earth revolves around the sun. It did so while men thought the opposite, or had no thoughts on the matter at all. It revolves now. It will continue as long as the system and the bodies continue their relative states and motions.

Two plus two equaled four before any animal could add. They always will.

What we can say that is true, and not open to refutation, is what we can state as having been true as our image reveals in the past, present and future that image connotes. Such truth is true irrespective of man's found and correct image.

A second sort of truth is time-fixed. Much that is true in the previous category may appear in this second one, but not all. The United States of America is true, now, and real and accurately imaginable in many ways. But it did not always exist and it doubtless will not exist forever or even, perhaps, for a next century. We hold a vast amount of such *temporary* categories of truth, with reason. But few of us distinguish between the first class of truth and the second. Many people equate both. The game called football is as real in most minds as the truth that visible stars are suns. But football is a recent development and the nature of its rules keep shifting, too, stars change but all reality changes. I find quibble here facetious. Unless we make the effort to distinguish between enduring realities and realities of temporal sorts, we are liable to great confusion and error. Most of us are badly scrambled in that way.

The third category in which we hold images many of us believe are true is established by the use of faith, in the broadest sense of "faith." This territory is composed of beliefs and "convictions" that lie outside of time and human reach. They include all religious formulations, heaven, hell, and God and gods and afterlife. They are our superstitions. They are areas which we will ignore or not allow investigation of on the grounds of personal conviction. They are hypothesized in ways that make demonstration impossible, proof be-

yond grasp, examination out of the question. For they do not
exist as realities in the manner of the other two kinds of
truth. They are wholly imagined and cannot be shown real
now in the past or in the future: they are merely presumed
real by their owners.

Much, if not most, of the images human beings use for
basic value—measurements lie in that territory, or, more accurately, non-territory, a mythic, invented and merely alleged
territory. And, unfortunately, most human beings regard the
contents of that faked region as truer than the other pair of
truths and even transcendent over them.

Not only religious beliefs but many others occupy most
inner landscapes. Among them is that long-standing and still-
general notion that man can conquer nature. Among them
is the idea that we are so superior to other life forms as to be
discrete and also that we have a right to use them (and all
things) as we wish at any moment. Among them is another
idea I have noted, the belief that man owns what tangible
matter he merely is allowed to use in his one lifetime.

The last is as dangerous and prevalent a delusion as any
of the others. No man owns anything or can; neither does
any group of men, corporation or nation. What we think of
as possession is temporary because the possessors are mortal.
We die and then what we believed we owned passes to
others. While we had the use of it, *all* we ever had, we may
have altered it. But we could not destroy it since matter is
not subject to destruction. We can will it to heirs but we
cannot control property of heirs from the grave.

How we used what we only imagined we owned will be
determined by the rest of our beliefs and whether they are
true or false.

Ecology has made that circumstance plain.

It shows that the way men have made use of all they
imagined they owned, was *only* use, *not* possession. By evad-

ing that truth, men have given little heed to the results of their uses of resources and they give little, still, to what they are now using. Today we act in ways certain to pass on to posterity a planet so devastated its wounds will bear witness to our near-infinite errors of viewpoint about possession and time. For it is our temporal delusion that leads to that dreadful fallacy about ownership of real territory.

What men have thought of as progress, then, was misconceived owing to an inner territorial error in our images of time and its relation to truth.

What a man and all men own is their skin and its contents. Everything beyond that hide is beyond human possession and at most, open to use.

Marxists may applaud this thought as valid because private ownership is their devil. But collective ownership is exactly as wrong an image of reality, an altered version of the same inner blindness.

If man were able to possess anything beyond his body as his property and not something more that is part of nature, he would be able to take that property along with himself, forever.

But if man had realized he owns nothing but has only its use, he would have taken charge of his usable domain in a proper manner.

Man never did. He does not, now. Rather, a few men are only beginning to be aware of the fact that he hasn't taken command of what he uses.

Gregory Bateson said it all:

Nobody's in charge.

No person or persons.

Nature's in charge, utterly, irrevocably and unchangeably.

Nature therefore makes the final appraisal of all man's acts. Nature gives the ultimate verdict.

Man's image of his technological "progress" will demand

whatever may be due for violations of the ruling laws of nature, those "first category truths," payable now, or tomorrow, as it was yesterday.

No political, religious, economic, social or other concepts that are imagined without absolute regard to the laws of nature are reliable or meaningful and most such are quicksands, however firm they are imagined.

No psychology is worth a whistle that does not contemplate man as the animal he is, and as one with the mistaken right-wrong value-systems he now employs, systems that do not distinguish among the three means we use to stake out territory we call truth (the one, correct, the second, correct at present, the third, mere dreams without any relation to territorial reality). Time is the proper criterion for truth.

It is perhaps interesting and, to me, an amusing coincidence that as I edited the above (1970) three major groups of liberal-intellectual professionals—social scientists, political scientists and academic psychologists—had recently experienced illustrative chaos. Radicals on the left and black radicals played havoc with the American Psychological Association during their convention at Provincetown. The same sort of thing happened at the San Francisco convention of the American Sociological Association, where a "post-behavioral revolution" against *that* obsolete school of sociological psychology was openly faulted, with brilliance and vehemence. And the entire doctoral scheme was dynamited in a report sponsored by the American Political Science Association.

In a just-arrived communication from Harold Goodwin, a friend, I find a quotation from Sigmund Koch that pretty well sums up the underlying cause of all this uproar in those three powerhouses of the LIE:

Psychology, Koch says, is "pseudo-knowledge with the

stipulation that psychology be adequate to science outweighed that it be adequate to man."

The reference is, of course, to academic psychology, behaviorism, in short. It must first suit psychologists, not truth.

The sudden, three-fold assault on the very cathedrals and catechisms of my lifelong antagonists, the liberals and intellectuals of the academy and the academy-birthed professions doesn't mean any more, per se, than any other confrontation of enraged student-non-student-professor bands of over-age adolescents. The people who raised the roof were, I gathered, just superficially provoked by relatively minor fallacies and irritants.

There was no sign among those involved of a major gain in values or any essential enlightenment. Nobody requested an inquiry into the laws of nature as a means to find what changes were needed to substitute a true valid base for the gassy follies that are believed to anchor these disciplines, psychology with political and social "science." If the insurrections result in shifts, they are just other directed drifts in that ridiculous balloon where the myopic LIE Passepartouts see man as the source of all truth and as living outside nature so, in effect, supernatural, or doctorially divine.

The idea that reality seen below may consist of three provinces, one real, one real but only as a present, the third, empty of any substance and all those diffcrences owing to time-use and/or mis-use, is far, far from their balloon-basket notice. And all of them use their binoculars wrong-end-to.

Their eruptions and divisions are symptomatic of the dimly seen queasiness below but they don't realize they helped in that sense of what is wrong is not a beginning of wisdom but only an arrival at that one place where wisdom might begin. (Activists please note).

These, LIE people, are the ones who have shaped the territorial myths of the young rebels and revolutionaries.

They followed Pope: *The proper study of mankind is man,* never reading more.

For half a century, students of other animals have shown that dogma to be asinine.

It hardly scratches the surface as a proper study for man, of man.

It is not a wonder, then, that youthful feeling—anger, fear, rage, righteousness, every sort of hot ire is man-focused and now—timed.

For the source of the young people's rage, their alienation, their identity-search, is but reality as this self-appointed Authority surveyed it, in too limited a frame of reference for cogent use. And this is the source of the knowledge and of belief, such as they are, of the parents of the young activists: Liberals and intellectuals and affluent, too, nearly all those fathers and mothers of the piggery.

A seeming paradox is now explained. Students who demand "relevant" studies feel those the LIE offers are irrelevant; but the ideas of *relevant* studies put forward by the young objectors are not gains but actually more distant from what is relevant even than what they abhor and reject.

They are the third generation or, at least, the second, well-heeled, of liberal-intellectual "thinkers" whose whole thought begins and ends in my third, or "atemporal," non-dimension. Here, it is a territory called man seen as *all* the significant territory, in all time, without reference to man's ancestral and animal past, his species-span as animal, his animal future or the possibility of evolution there.

The proper study of mankind is *life.*

Biology, anyone?

17. The Crisis in Identity: Episode Four

When we identify ourselves with our species exclusively, or even mainly, and do not consult the knowledge available about other breeds, we have met and failed in one more crisis. It may be difficult to look at a goat and see yourself as its cousin. But if you cannot manage that, you will have lost a major route to self-indentification.

Anthropology, comparative anthropology and all other genuine sciences of man are limited in that same way. It is impossible for men to extrapolate, from all that can be learned about men, and men only, concepts, laws, social premises, or economic or political laws meaningful enough to suffice for self-knowing, let alone, how to behave.

What I have been showing in its broadest terms is that the rapid expansion of science and scientific knowledge faced man with a challenge that men have evaded generally and that where they have accepted scientific knowledge they have done so in bits and pieces. They have applied what data offered profit, material benefit, health, longevity and entertainment, without regard to the rest.

Inasmuch as they have yet, after a century, entered evolution into their acts and incorporated its immense territory into their prior holdings, with the requisite junking and revision, it is not surprising that they have failed to accept and incorporate numerous less-germane-seeming discoveries, as great and, in fact, real and as change-demanding. What Einstein stated is beyond them. So is nearly all the data of all pure science as it stands or grows. They do not, as I said, even know what science is.

The identity crisis precipitated by science differs in result from the more primitive ones I have discussed.

Faced with the new knowledge and its constant increase, men did not invariably fail to measure up to the need. A large number incorporated into their beliefs a fair amount of science, and especially of the physical sciences. But biology, the so-called "life sciences," was not much learned or used to correct prior holdings, where biology required the biggest property-shifts. To most who know a little of it, biology is seen as the science of all things living *except* man.

Older realms of conviction prevailed there. Men rejected and will reject what biology learned and goes on learning by denying its importance to man and his ongoing, still-corrupt self-description. That the biology of worms has any integral relationship to the biology of men, very few can accept and employ to correct the worm-belittler. The behavior of ducks is cogent for men as a description of whatever men do that is similar with a great part of all we do! But people who have achieved such new broadening of their prior subjective kingdoms still represent a very small minority of the total population.

The physical sciences were merely exploited by technology, (every reader must repeat till it is memorized) but all other realms of knowledge were skipped. Further (to repeat *that!*), the LIE undertook to don the trappings of science by counting, by measuring and by silly, statistical endeavors presumed to give their powerful realms scientific status.

Science is knowledge and knowledge of how to get more. The tools of research are not "science." The arts-and-crafts members of the LIE mistook the implements for the method. They never could be scientists by that loan.

What value has an opinion poll about air pollution taken among people ignorant of photosynthesis by scholars who have no meterology, radiation physics or algology? Indeed, if such every-multiplying pseudo-disciplines were real, there could not be a dozen schools of economics, political science and the rest. There could be only one apiece. But nobody in the LIE had a baseline except mankind and mankind as the liberal intellectual saw himself, too, often.

In such a territorial vacuum it is not surprising that the early words of the behavioral folks were hailed as the Final Solution to All Intelligent Process, but the LIE: reflex and operant conditioning are so exceedingly *simple* (they thought). And being simple has marked them since that day. They were also able to remain mechanists but get away from the Cartesian horror. A non-man when tortured may scream but doesn't feel pain because it has no "mind," Descartes revealed and widely peddled. Behaviorism let the primitives off that hook. But it was still good, ringing, basic, easy mechanism, and the people not interested in natural science certainly did need those characteristics for anything they could call "scientific" and work at in a "scientific" manner.

The inferences they drew have been amply recorded, here. How much that happened constantly everywhere, but failed to fit their transcendent machine-faith and had to be ignored, I think is now equally clear. How odious the results of their inferences and the ensuing applications have become is visible as much of the rebel scene, and the square one, too. But *why* and how they managed to act that way for half a century, and do so still in posses, when surrounded by evidence of their stupidity, not to their treason as observers and logicians, is a little bit harder to explain.

Since the young activists and leftists have this same built-in capacity for willful unrealism and passionate self-deception, for professing omniscience when actually not even talking sense or thinking at all, I shall take a shot at solving their inner shambles, or opening the bear-trap they say is not there and not holding them down.

We are all engaged in a game of one-upmanship.

Maybe we don't play hard or hope to score much if at all, and certainly, nobody can play fairly every minute. Usually, we play by wrong rules, which is disastrous. We play by a rule that seems to say that by virtue of birth on some team, or as a player on another chosen later, we must at least do better than *somebody* else. Low man is out. Even in the goose-pecking orders, though, the omega animal occasionally gets a shot at moving up a few steps or even getting to be beta and, to its joy, though this is rare, alpha.

If we had no more imagination than geese, and inasmuch as we do have about the parallel set of instincts, the above way of playing would be right. However, being imaginative and able, in consequence, to imagine ourselves and even to imagine we could improve our awareness and so, our score as selves, we needn't bother with the outside pecking orders, much: enough to eat and so on, as a limit. The real game men and only men can play (to their glory) is inner, the self *with and against* the self, to move ourselves up in that open-ended pecking order.

So we come to identify crisis Number Four in a new design. How much of what's known are you ready to add to what you know, or think you know, so as to have an alpha-approaching identity? *That* is the whole human game, because once an animal begins to imagine itself, it will not have any other player to compete with. Where your mind exists there is nobody home but you, if you are, that is.

Lower animals had no such "I" awareness. Primitive men

identified themselves so completely with the tribe that they found the first person singular incomprehensible. You, modern man, man for ages, slowly found he was an *I*. Unfortunately, the experience is, again, a recent thing in the evolution of species. And just because it is recent, by my loose reasoning or casual grasp of analogue (so frowned on by scholars but so enormously helpful in their dilemmas), our *I* awareness hasn't yet begun to sit as an easy crown. Ancient philosophers rued their shut-in solitude, their inescapable territory of "I" almost as self-pityingly as a million under-thirties decry their alienation.

It is a real condition. That's the price we pay for having the only capacity there is for super-fun aside from physical pleasures and emotional joys. I will put so much bend on logic as to suggest that super-fun is what the self is *for*. It is meant to be its own best friend and most formidable opponent, in a game which can be started by its own signal and played to an infinitely high score. Nothing like that ever evolved here previously and nothing of the like has been found, in cosmos, yet, anyhow. The rules for the game are very stringent and playing it well is very much like but harder than playing all other known games at once, were that feasible. The object is to win the clearest possible image of reality. This means changing each player's real estate as new information requires. It demands the utmost honesty of self-image and of outer, too, that you can manage, whatever the cost of that in *amour-propre*. Such costs can be borne without limit, however, since the more reality and real self you win the more humble you will become. The highest scores are not hurt by learning of errors but glad of that chance for more points.

Corollary: Every evidence of arrogance of people under thirty, especially, is a sign of a small inflated by the stale breath of somebody else.

The self that scores highest knows best how relatively few points it earned because it knows how much more to find.

Life is, for most, a game of one-upmanship, me versus you-all.

Our million-year or two-million-year idea of what man is cannot let man easily learn the real game. Each nonhuman animal has a built-in right-wrong scoring system, arranged for a species end as I've already stated. And man has the innate need for such a system, too, but he will settle for a system he *thinks* is that kind. Since he has a consciousness of an emotionally powerful kind, but since he did not and does not take his model from the rest of the animal kingdom to which he belongs, he was and is able to make terrible errors about his right-wrong system, even as he erred in other ways at crisis points.

To him, as he has imagined himself, the need for a "moral system" could and did produce innumerable systems, none of them correct (as shown by results and as they are proven, universally, in other species), but all of them acceptable to his corrupted sense of his self, at least, for a time. Man had merely to *seem* to know right and wrong, he felt. For other animals, not to *know* would result in desperate frustration, confusion and life-aim failure. The result for man is that, too. But he is not aware of it, yet.

Instead, his every territory of belief and conviction has an associated right-wrong system as fallacious as the territory it is designed to service. And so long as he assumes he merely needs to seem right and not to seem wrong to himself (and also to his tribe or community), that unexamined desire to seem right and seem to know wrong, too, causes him to defend any accepted inner territory, however idiotic, by all means at hand. What it is believed to be, in his opinion, is correct. And his need to protect it as the most valid of all such idols and systems is absolute—because it is his system.

He is his manufactured god—and that invisible deity is served according to its "moral law," that the worshiper accepts with the invented package.

Every man's sense of inner security reposes in his self, his artifact and in the presumed reliability of whatever its attached value system may be. Outside of man the system is innate and as near perfect as nature requires. Little wonder that man has the continuing sense of a need, for the biological imperative. Little wonder, too, that in his identity crises he flunked every time! For he saw the "need" as personal.

Aware imagination could not be evolved with a rigid, ancestral ethos—a right-wrong code and rituals for defending the owner's turf and for gaining his place in the peck order. To be aware, to have unlimited powers of image-making, connotes an open-ended potential. *Genus homo* was and is obliged to invent himself and dream up the rules of the game of existence. Without that obligation he would not have been different from the moral but unimaginative rest.

If we were to think of the evolutionary process as purposeful and imagine that the evident rise of biological complexity *meant* anything, we could envisage man in an interesting way. He, the current end-product (or summit?) of the long series of form-shifts would represent a biological leap far *greater* than the crazy dream of divinity. The notion that there is some "supreme being" somewhere or other, who (or which) is "in charge" of destiny is thus tawdry compared to the truth. With man, evolution ventured a new, infinite and terrifying chance. It created in a being the capacity to take charge of evolution itself, on the planet and perhaps elsewhere, in a long run. Such is truth as shown by that parable.

This is a wonderful thought.

And it is a true thought. We do have the power to manage evolution. Where other animals are concerned we have used it widely, domesticating some species, exterminating many, and sensing an evolved power greater than they possess but, of course, sensing it as separate and superior and unrelated to them. Even at this late day the suggestion of taking any responsibility for our own breed still sends shudders through the minds of the near-universally heathen. Control birth? Death? Euthenasia? Fumbling with genes? Culling defectives? Limiting the numbers of offspring?

God, no!

Who would *decide* such questions?

Well, nature will decide them all, and shortly, unless man undertakes the task for which he was fitted when he emerged in the olden dawn. He has largely rejected a mere image of himself that could allow and implement this necessary use of his imagination to employ truths-found and logics-invented for the improvement of his kind. The naked potential was so great, so inflating, so readily corrupted to furnish false pride that man never saw the true pride he could earn.

Surely, there must be a right-wrong morality for human beings, a *single* code! A means to a proud breed!

And, plainly, it should be based on the same principle that leads to the ethological end, a best-attainable chance for the next generation of the species. Such is the life process everywhere else. Such is its only means of continuing and continuing to evolve. Such is biological "immorality" and whoever swipes a piece of that to invent a personal life after death is a traitor to his kind, to his mind, to the imagination he thus has corrupted, to reason and, were there any God, to that God.

We serve this slightly acknowledged part-real ethos in a fashion. Everybody wants their own offspring to have advantages they did not. Even the LIE has its "humanism" and "humanitarian" code. But the laws of nature, which the LIE ignores, have nothing to do with that brand of humanism or that sort of allegedly humanitarian "ethic." Nature is in charge and nature offers neither special status nor tenure to man. Nature does not give a damn for man, as such. And unless man devotes himself to learning and obeying the laws of nature, he is doomed. The rules are adamant and clear and cannot be compromised by religious amendments. They cannot yield to skepticism, either or any view that assumes the nonbeliever is right for not having belief.

One-upmanship is that same folly of the group as it is of the individual. Playing life as politics, nationalism, as an economic race or even as noncompetitors, in the way the scientists have played, is, forever, playing for dismal ends by stupid rules. But as long as men identify themselves with such self-views they will not become men. Their rites of offense and defense will be reasonless and murderous and their orders of status will be absurd.

How does this constant and complete blunder so endlessly occur? Why do the Christian legions act precisely like the followers of Baal or Mao? How can a horde of people under thirty claim to be more knowledgeable than their predecessors and prove otherwise by behaving like farts?

Ethology has shown the moral equivalent in all other species of what men have never exhibited. What, then, so steadily hides our potential and keeps us in our station of the least honorable animal?

Can man's amorality be understood?

It is even possible that the following phenomenon, recently described and amply documented by the ethologists, may be a human phenomenon, too, and if it is, no moral teacher and no educator has even the start on an understanding of how men learn and so, how to teach.

The phenomenon is called "imprinting" and was first described and demonstrated, I think, by Lorenz.

Whether or not it be true of man, it is a proposition of an

order and a strangeness (for most men) of new-found kinds
that do relate to man, help define him, describe him more
correctly in various fashions and so, a proposal of possible
use in his identity search.

A new sort of question arises here, if man is seen an
imprinted holder of inner real estate, some of which is valid;
some, mistaken; and much, beyond proof or examination.
This question:

Why does a man who earnestly, unreservedly and sin-
cerely tries to revise his inner scene to match new knowledge,
so often *fail?* Why does another fail even to try?

That is the problem as it was posed by my friend Henry
Kyburg, author of *The Philosophy of Science* and a man with
graduate degrees in both those areas.

He had tried to teach the new math to math teachers,
adults, who wanted and needed to learn it for professional
purposes. They were able to understand the basic ideas of
"sets," in due course. But they could not employ that information to solve problems, to teach or to think with, in effect.

Why?

The example and the question stand for man's most
pervading and perplexing incapacity, a breakdown of the
individual ability to use imagination beyond a specific point,
of which there are millions of points for mankind. The wish
and will to advance in the mind where some specific opportunity is seen, doesn't always suffice for the end. Even
when the data that furnish the base for added learning are
actually learned, the lesson is useless for application. We
often cannot yield up inner territory we see is false even
though we may try our best. The facts are accepted but are
not of functional worth.

What is the wall we cannot climb or penetrate or even
identify as that barrier, and merely encounter, without a
sufficient sense of its nature to pass beyond?

Let the reader reckon with it.

Man is an animal, I said, and he knows.

But does the fact become the central insight into who he is and what he should and should not do?

Does he see man as the sport man is, the deviate, the one without morals, the limitless aggressor who is alone and terrible and doomed if he remains that? Does he see that, as animal, he depends on the biosphere exactly as others do? Does he see that his only real meaning refers to what mankind may mean in his future and that his life-meaning is gauged either by his contribution to that actually unimaginable end, or else by his hindrance to that undefinable hope? Does his obdurate stand prevent him, and as many other men as he can influence, from discovering what the real meaning, morals and potential of animals were and are?

He tries. He can't budge.

What's the block? The barrier? Why are we able to assume we are reasonable and yet act as if we had no reason whatever?

A new-hatched duck takes the first thing that moves as its parent. A booby will nest only at that point from which it made its first flight. Those "beliefs" were imprinted on the two breeds—for one, at "birth," the other, at "adolescence." They control the birds' lives after the event. And even though we know nature provides all creatures with a built-in motor-pattern, a suitable "moral" code, for the same end, here, the system can be seen to fail. A duckling that met a wolf, first, might never carry on the duck-species, and a booby that was first air-borne from a spiked fence could not later nest there and so, never would reproduce.

Is *man* subject to such processes?

The child at five or six has a "personality" sufficiently fixed to affect its remaining years. We think of that as owing to "training"; but how can we then explain that the yes-no, right-wrong, good-naughty, true-false instruction of a pre-schooler is fixated so firmly? We may identify the engraving tools as adult instruction but how do we define the brain that was so arbitrarily engraved and so permanently that much of the message is mistaken but not subject to later correction.

We know, too, that during puberty the young human being passes through a "mystical" stage in which the psyche is subject to impressions that cannot be related to genital maturation. The adolescent will seek strange company, briefly hold peculiar ideas and complete or fail in the struggle to leave the nest—that battle of fathers and sons, mothers and daughters which must be waged and also must be won for in-dividuation and even, for mere mental health, in later years. So here, again, the already once-graven brain becomes plastic in a second manner and takes a new set of messages often as indelible as the first.

And a final setting of the plastic likely follows: biological growth is complete and the individual begins to die. Still, he or she is not always and not inevitably stuck with all the inward images that have been stamped on the brain. Some imagination is left operational and so most or all people can perceive new truths and change accordingly. Some can change even when the truths repudiate the prior print.

Whatever worth the concept of imprinting has (or lacks) here, a similar effect is readily observable. Much of our right-wrong index was programmed by age six. And much more programming may occur at adolescence. It is a period, cer-tainly, for trial and error in many regions of ideas and values. In most youths, error is often not just a result of several trials, but the finally accepted result, correct or no.

Here, however, man exhibits a different way of behaving from that of lesser creatures, as he calls them. "Trial and error" is the behaviorist's term. Konrad Lorenz shattered the concept by stating it correctly as, "trial and success." The revision is vital for understanding and it is demonstrated by the simple, statistical fact. If nonhuman "learning" were the product of trials and of errors continued up to some random and correct act of a successful sort, no creature would learn the right acts. The incidence of possible errors for all is too great. And, as I've said, too many failures will not lead to endless trials but simply end in frustration and trial-refusal.

If man were built that way, he would have an equivalent capacity for recognizing the right act, in his search for it, after a similarly-limited number of trials properly-vectored to allow man, like the others, a successful effort falling within a range smaller than the frustrating number.

Maybe the capability still exists in our breed. If, perhaps, we had achieved a set of ethical rules suited to our reality and to our place in nature, we might see the ancient phenomenon in operation. But as long as the assorted "moral" rules we employ to raise (and "educate") children remain in effect, and as long as other systems of the same perverted kind dominate adolescence, we cannot hope to discern the process. Nowadays we can but infer it, and only by noting its results in reverse: the terrible consequences of what surely must be a plastic character of man, forcefully imprinted with moral errors.

The question that rises from that view, admittedly an imaginative one, is simple and perhaps cogent without the features I have invented.

Since the human child and adolescent seen "as-if imprinted" with "moral" systems that prevent the victim from later correction, we must ask, is there a way to "imprint" the child with permanent plasticity?

Can we raise open-minded people?

Yes? How does it then happen that some adults *are* very

open-minded all their lives and able to change innumerable "beliefs" to new and different beliefs, as evidence comes in requiring that? I think that sort of adult must have gone through a number of experiences, prior to age five, or six, and for at puberty, if not in both periods, by which he or she was "imprinted" with a sense of the *value* of retaining an open-mind. Further, such experiences must have appeared to be enjoyable, rewarding, fit, morally virtuous.

Since children learn from parents or other adults by their acts, their counsel, these broad-minded and permanently-educable adults must either have witnessed the inner growth (by opinion-shift and by new learning) of some adult who felt the process valuable, or, just possibly, by an opposite "lesson." Growing up under adults who are so close-minded that a little kid can see their mistakes might, at least, cause under-five individuals to try for and succeed in finding the other and only valuable way of using the self-image, by open-mindedness.

What does "all that" have to do with grade school math teachers who can learn the concepts of new math but not how to apply them? Do I mean their parents were a-mathematical? Or that some teen-age pal stamped into them at a critical moment the notion that math was only a headache and without practical value?

Yes . . . and no.

Somewhere in the past of these blocked minds a door closed. Or one wasn't opened that should have been. Somewhere, an inner value-system was fixed at a level that led the prisoner to assume himself or herself able to go "this far" but "no farther." That the block should fall where math is concerned is not the necessary point. What fell was an im-printed limit, artificial and crippling, and its effect as a barricade in math may merely be the exhibition of a "displacement act" due to a deeper cause, one, perhaps inadmissible and so, displayed in a symbolic way to satisfy a demand by a *proxy* which then serves as a seeming evasion of acknowledging the actual barricade to others and even one's self.

This is speculative.

So is all we do, say, think, believe and know.

Once we take the proper view of man as a member of the animal kingdom we may find our observations of those relatives useful. In this discussion of right-wrong systems appropriate for each species, there is more room for thought than the behavorists found. Let me review a little.

Knowledge of what's right may be enough to connote the wrong acts. What's "wrong" may—or may not—follow from information of the correct move. But to think no such knowledge is innate, that it is either gained by trial and error, or taught by adults to the young, and so, entirely mechanical and automatic, is not to look enough.

Some creatures do have all their needed moral guidance inscribed in reflexes, or, innate in source.

Others may learn by trial and success, or by that, aided in many ways, such as by code-marks, coded sounds and the like, that reduce the trials for success.

Many are instructed by adults. They ape what they are shown.

But all these must have an innate ability to learn whatever they must know that is not automatic. That ability cannot be a mere negative that, exposed enough times, will finally get the right photograph. For how would such a photograph identify the correct print when endless near-right acts and objects may be present? Or when the proper one has nothing to do with any prior experience?

Finally, there is man.

He, too, innately "knows" a right-wrong system is essential for living. But he is "adaptive." He can thrive in many different environs so he can and must be able to learn varied patterns of what is right to do, what's wrong, what to avoid, and so on. If he had one image of himself germane to his kind, his ability to adapt would be limited to that of the other creatures in that state. The ablest of those adapts only slowly to new conditions and only within environmental limits of a relatively narrow range. That range is extended, if ever, by changing the animal, itself. Man, even there, has undergone some changes for that end, as in color.

All pre-human methods of knowing and of learning are sufficiently effective for maintaining the species while the external conditions permit that. Mistakes are made in every breed by individuals. But, statistically, the motor patterns are effective enough and, usually, more than enough so that, without external checks, myriads of species could and would overwhelm their niches.

But what man has found essential, so far, is but *a* "morality," any sort, even one that may, in the moderate run, destroy his posterity.

Elsewhere, I have set forth the proposition that man's cultural "evolution" has done exactly that!

The higher the culture, I pointed out, the more of its members must be freed from labor for survival, so they can provide the "cultural" additions. That, in turn, means "progress" in a society stems from technological "advance." Only that way can men provide people who have any chance to develop arts, sciences, religions, armies, political systems, laws, luxuries and all else that we see as cultural.

That much is self-evident. So is my next step. The technological advances required for cultural "gains" will, by definition, accelerate the exploitation of the environment, deplete resources and intrude on eco-systems, unless and until such a culture understands and abides by the laws of ecology. None ever did. None does.

From that it follows inevitably that, the higher a culture the sooner it will destroy its supportive environs. The more effective a society's technology, then, the shorter its existence will be, however, "higher" its cultural estate in the time span. There are modifications of the principle; but no flaws appear in it that anyone has yet found. What it means, if correct, is that man will never create a society with an open-ended future until and unless he establishes a culture in which his technology is matched to the people-load and the per capita goods and services which an open-ended future will define.

Our own, very recent and explosive technology has already satisfied the principle sufficiently to show that, unless we revise everything, and soon, we shall have done ourselves in at the predictable shortest interval of all past cultures.

This concept is valuable for its indication of the morality, the right-wrong system man must follow, replacing all others with that one, even to hope to persist for another century or so.

But no such "morality" is taught the human infant-child-adolescent-or-adult. Even though many of us have recognized the damage lately done to the life-supporting biosphere as pollution, as harm to various eco-systems, nobody much has seen the process the historic consequence of man's ceaseless failure to place himself properly in nature and act as that locus demands.

We operate still from the simple drive to have a right-wrong program, but any sort or any one that will not clearly cause quick cultural collapse. Whether such a system is Christian or Hindu, Moslem or Maoist, rightist or leftist, determinist or based on "free will"—even if it be a nihilism, an absence of morals or Sartre's silly notion that life is and has got to be absurd, it achieves nothing of value.

All such systems are worthless because none has any bearing on existence in a future. Whoever believes any such program will be misidentified and his efforts at righteousness, even, will be pointless or, oftener, invidious and deadly for everybody to follow.

If, then, as I have inferred, we are a life form that is subject to "imprinting" at an early stage, not to mention, at a second, later period, it does not seem probable that we shall soon jettison the erroneous beliefs and their attached ideas of good and evil to replace them with the correct set of values, the good of men to come after us. We shall go on for some long while stamping infancy with the hideous images and "laws" that we derived in our efforts to "improve" our identity by falsifying the palpable facts.

Even the hope that parents and other adults will soon start imprinting tots with the virtue of open-mindedness is bleak. For what father, what mother, however eager to provide more "advantages" than theirs, will then furnish them with minds open enough so their children will have new identities and identities that—in the view of almost every living adult—are seen as inferior for their overriding inclusion of man as animal?

Of course, the intense and pervasive reluctance, there, is owing to man's perpetual misidentification of animals and man's perverted idea of their actual nature. He has switched reality in this basic area of being and attributed to animals all the amoral, stupid, brutal and utterly evil characteristics that man, and only man, exhibits.

To ask, then, why human beings are unable to learn some new and improved image of reality, or why they are able to learn only one image but not how to revise it when necessary, is to ask a final question.

It is to ask why man is not rational, or open-minded, teachable or remotely moral in the universal and one true sense of the term.

The answer seems to be that he has exerted, from his dim beginnings as man, an immense pressure against learning, against reality, against truth, against common sense, against logic, and against every element and aspect of these that would or might interfere with his ugly-god, nasty-logical image of himself.

That is what he worships as god.

Those who know only people-derived data about people, the LIE members, are in the same class with fire-worshipers, animists, Papists, Presbyterians, servants of Ra and Christian Scientists. For all such teaching and belief prevent thought, limit honesty, banish integrity and gain nothing but the artificial arrogance men everywhere exhibit and the mad fears that are the price for that.

We are like a species of spider. We inject the venom of our moral notions into our progeny and they become paralyzed to a degree that allows them to move and live and be only as their paralysis allows, a condition that requires handing the venom to their next generation.

One toxic culture follows another as the venom kills off each old society. The poisons grow subtler and the cultures more elaborate. Most of what most citizens do is no longer even related to the work of the minority that supplies the basic needs for all. The priestly castes and their temples, the artisans and scientists, the engineers and appliers of science, the teachers and lawyers, the great majority become, in that sense, parasitical on the workers. But the workers have technologies for their duties and whether these arise before the cultural innovations, or stem from them, matters not.

For their combined effects set up higher and higher cultures, exploiting the biosphere more swiftly and enormously thus ensuring a quicker doom. The sands of time drift over their stone cadavers. The higher they were, the faster they

exhausted vital resources and turned their green and living
sustenance into desert. Some of them found ways to prolong
the interval, but none, to give it any hope of a continuum.

Their members conquered other peoples and took their
resources, ravishing their environment. Slaves furnished the
most skill and brawn at the lowest cost. Trade supplied
products both participants desired, at a pro rata environmental expense to each. New technology found better means to
gather or get necessities (and luxuries) from the additional
mineral and plant and animal sources their invention enables
men to exploit but all such achievements only postponed
the ultimate fate, the inevitable self-ruin of the culture.

Nobody was watching the ledgers of nature.

No culture owned a moral system that had anything to do
with the laws of nature.

They were spiders, always, races and nations of a species
that continued for thousands of years in an effort to sustain
images of man as superior to all other life, apart, above,
utterly other. The images for these serial beliefs changed,
the cultures grew complex, but the change was only in the
poison. It became subtler, but the subtler, or cleverer, the
swifter-acting.

We call that long record a history of cultural "evolution"
and we say it reveals man's "adaptability."

The awful truth is other. The more culturally advanced
our societies were, the sooner they came to an end. We have
not yet been adaptive in any way. Every achievement
that we regard as progress or that was so seen, in the past
by the self-styled achievers, was in ultimate effect, counter-
adaptive. It killed off that batch of progressives.

Now, our "adaptivity" has allowed us to people every
likely niche on earth. Our technology is so fecund that
continental resources are exhausted in a single lifetime and
the casual by-products of our ingenious applications of bits

and pieces of science contaminate the biosphere as a whole. We are beginning to sicken and die of the culture we have evolved, this highest, ever, so swiftly self-poisoned in the little time since the Industrial Revolution. If we had the equivalent of the ethology of lice we would not have embarked upon this now-demand for instant-gratifications with its price tag of doomsday for all men, the innocent with the guilty, and the due-date perhaps already set, insofar as we have determined.

But people are still going to church.

People still believe in the "economic man" of the left, new or old.

The LIE still instructs its students with its non-disciplines and its anti-knowledge that the shamans derive from the one source that, for them, is proper—themselves, mankind—not, life.

Before it was called "ecology," the inexorable laws of life that derived from physics and chemistry and that rule biology had a different name.

"Biotic economy," they called it, in the twenties, at my university.

Not any value-system used by anybody on earth, save the people involved knowledgeably with "biotic economy," even *relates* to the real cost-accounting by which man lives, or dies, as he has done in his past cultures and is about to do in Olympic-record time, with this one. Nearly all the ruling value-systems are religious or political and so, utterly unrelated to the real system and usually so perverse and deviant as to make the true laws invisible to all the diverse billions of dupes.

And so it goes, in the mortal words of Kurt Vonnegut.

18. The Sons and Daughters as Mothers and Fathers

Now, nearing the end of this book, I am overwhelmed by the absurdity and despair of that predicament.

What is still manuscript will be irrevocable print when next I see it; for I do not much edit that frozen river of words. I leaf through the marred typescript and as the pages fall I do not read but only remember how long ago the first one rolled free and I know these later sheets, these blotted, altered, pen-scratched and scribbled drifts of paper have had all the advantages editors could give them and all I've managed, too.

I often wonder at this nearing instant of commitment how other writers feel. Do they, like me, have a sense, as absurd as it is depressing, that no book is ever completed? Do others, as they type those two words, "The End," realize they have ended nothing but merely reached the point at which they have given up? A point where patience ran out, of author or publisher, or where the schedules so aptly provided the end called "deadline?"

Do other writers know they quit and didn't finish? When their first edition arrives do they always see how this sentence, that chapter, this idea, that figure could and should have been improved? It happens to me forever; and once I've read my first edition I rarely read it again. There are so many faults! My only bearable reaction is to close this one—and hope, next time, I can do better.

This is truly absurd because, at the moment, and here, what will become a book is only manuscript, wide-open to amendment, rewriting, excision and addition and at no cost but continued effort and time. This brings the depressing factor: the decision is mine alone. It has to be and I have decided. I have not finished but quit.

The intensity of my emotions at such times is proportional to the earnestness, effort and thought I've given a manuscript. Here, it is extreme. How many chapters were cut out, how many others were redone, and (for the near-three-hundred pages remaining) how many marks made by editors, a little, by me, in their majority? A thousand! How conscious am *I* of what remains?

Here is another peculiar ludicrous aspect of the moment. For here, as often before, I have invited the very opprobrium I've recklessly employed.

This, all readers can say, is what *he* scoffs at: one-upmanship!

Sure.

And there is more to say than that, in the same way.

I've endeavored to bash the icons and to cut the stuffed heads of the same people who will most often and in the best places, evaluate my harangue, my sermon . . . I give them the terms.

Worse, still, by this use of this form, the "familiar essay," I have made it easier for every reader who finds cause to cavil, or for fury, to abort my purpose by ignoring it—by salvaging what dignity he can with some personal retort.

Philip Wylie is a son-of-a-bitch, for instance.

That may or may not be true but, either way, it has
nothing to do with the message. Such an effort furnishes a
false vent for wrath, only, or whatever may rise from the
written words that is attributed to me.

Finally, in this affair, I have used volumes of scholarly
material with accreditation and in a style that scholarship
forbids. But modern criticism, in reaction to erudite pedantry,
holds its opposite and extreme pose. The continued apoth-
eosis of Anglo-Saxon derivatives and the taboo of polysyllabic
words, in this late period of the twentieth century, is a
preposterous principle and one that typifies its inventors,
the membership of the LIE.

Most of what I regard as significant has come into being
long after the Angles and the Saxons vanished, by merging.
There's no useful four-letter-word for, say, deoxyribonucleac
acid though it does have an abbreviation: DNA. There, it is
a rarity and I could well have substituted endrocrinology,
photosynthesis or terms twice as long, every one of which
would leave the armed men at Hastings puzzled but every
one of which relates very importantly to everybody, now.

In the foregoing I intend neither apology nor a plea for
the reader's lenience. But I do feel a need to express certain
problems that are mine and are, probably, faults, in the main.
If a better vocabulary exists for my needs, it does not appear
in the writings of liberal intellectuals who are only that, and
without science. I can, with justification, condemn the critical
arrogance of their members, the frequent eagerness with
which such people accept books to review they are not
qualified to judge and then, for a few dollars, bury in cal-
umny, by cheatfulness.

By such acts they display their own ignorance, their dishonesty and that mean custom of using anybody's writing
to show off what their disciples and decent seekers of something worth reading, may accept as a useful opinion.

That is why I review my own books, internally, and repeatedly. The process may seem self-serving but it isn't, quite. It fails to sell a single copy. But it may persuade some buyers that their own opinion needn't be shaken by some negative bravura.

For whoever tries to write about liberty and exhibit some intellectual competence often needs a membership card in the LIE in order to get that mere acknowledgment. You can see I have no such counterfeit pass.

Before I sheathe my blade, then, let me try one or two last swipes.

The sons and daughters of mom will be the mothers and fathers of the next brood of Americans, and many are, already.

"Momism" as I described it nearly thirty years ago, referred to that mother whose method of child-raising was either by tyranny or bribery. Her incidence then was owing greatly to pop's abdication of parenthood. As tyrant, she embraced about the same ideas that are now pouring from the twisted lips of the Women's Lib militants. Mom knows what a man ought to be, but isn't, a God damned sight better than any male knows.

Clearly that mom, the "destroying" sort, was being replaced even back then by the other, the briber. And, plainly, a great many children managed to raise the bribe until it became all mom and pop possessed—the right to manage and control the family as they saw it. The other mom and her dank and rigid tyranny became the school teachers' role and there, under rules so petty and a system designed to quench the mind and decapitate reason, these kids got that second brand of momism.

Their rebellions are, as a result, not surprising in any way, however extreme, mad and self-destructive.

They are the ones I have mainly attacked here.

And, in one way, I have been unfair to the rest—the

square or straight, the great majority of people under thirty. For though they are following a tradition, they are following one that infinitely excels the non-traditions or leftist aims of such mutineers.

Their parents and their grandparents have achieved so much that is positive and marvelous, so much they originated, discovered, incorporated as reform into our society, that those sons and daughters who follow *them* and that tradition, can change again, in new and valuable ways, as leftists and militants cannot.

The dissident and activist, the militant and destructive under-thirties have proven that. They are out to get the establishment and system. They intend to ruin it, without any notion of what is to follow, which is nihilism. Or they would replace our bleeding and diminished liberty, but, still, the most liberty men own today, with Red rule. Extreme rightists have the same, if opposite-seeming aim: they want a Hitler and hitlers merely have the other face of stalins and maos, too.

The rebels, then, are rigidly dogmatic, nihilist or leftist. They cannot even relate to the slavery Communist doctrine imposes because it *is* a slave-system, and where it is in effect, it is *visible as slavery* to all but these blind and panicky nuts.

But above all, they fail to note, leftist or nihilist, hippie of any other copper-outer, what the current system and its establishment achieved in the last half-century that is both remarkable and virtuous. All that, they take for granted, consume, enjoy—and abuse, too, with never a notion that it was gained by the blood and sweat and guts of decent people, and so, might be advanced by *their* sons and daughters and could be advanced *only* by them. Their tradition is plastic. They can change, evolve, grow and make a better world and the record in their widely detested traditions is the proof. Nobody else has that potential.

But these square traditionalists cannot be burned, stoned, battered or bombed into change. Such means will merely make them become increasingly hostile to the attackers and to their motives, their nothing-will or their dogmatic, Red willfulness, that is relatively emptier than nothing. Driven far enough, these people will yield what they have believed and sustained, freedom, such as it was and is and they could better, merely to put down the bastard rabble.

There are signs, as I come to the end of this discussion, of some recovered sanity. A number of students are returning to democratic politics as a way for reforms no sensible citizen would but commend and desire. If they continue with that method and finally prevail over revolutionary attempts that are self-doomed, we shall, again, move ahead in our one possible manner.

But if young anger boils over anew and halts that effort, it will just bring more rounds of infamy on the part of youth and counterfire by "pigs" who have yet to kill a single mutineer, a fact the mental hoods never land, don't notice —but might well evaluate to all who's most pig.

It is difficult for a human being who has seen what Americans have added to the sum of human assets, inner and material, in this century, to tolerate those hordes of rebels who have no history (it would reveal their blunders) and take for granted what we gained and they now exploit, contemptuously. The gain is taken as if it were a birthright and they credit no one for what they first live by and then, would smash. Who's got a claim on *justice?*

They have no "new direction" because there is none better than the one we and our sires took and the one we try, still, to use as a guide. Their aims are mechanical, mere reaction. For "new directions" do not invariably provide progress that is an eternal verity and one readily deduced by watching Ping-Pong.

What, then, have I tried to say to show how we could opt this culture out of the endless, Toynbeean sequence of those that always rose and always fell? I'll try to sum it up.

For that end, I will use a term some finicky scholars abhor. But until or unless they find a better one, it's all we have. The word is, "instinct." If you will grant, for the sake of a brief construct, that the nature of man as *within* nature and *of* it, is valid—despite his efforts to deny that—then you may be able to imagine man as instinctual, and there, similar to all other life-forms.

If so, what is your concept of the *basic* instinct in our species?

Do you believe it is the "instinct for self-preservation?"

Or do you believe it even credible that man has an instinct for "survival after death?"

Finally, as I've repeatedly and doubtless too often noted, all other species are ordered by an "instinct" that comes, complete, with a set of right-wrong rules appropriate for each kind and that result, beyond denial, in lives devoted, however blindly, to one end, only, the provision of the best possible chance for the *survival of its species*.

Sooner or later, with the end accomplished by enough of the breed for the one purpose, all die. "Self-preservation," then, is but a passing and secondary requirement. Survival after death is ludicrous, for here, heaven and hell would be swarming with extinct bugs and shuddering with dinosaur tread, while people would be scarce.

If evolution has brought our species to a point where we can see the inviolable law, and, seeing it, discard our beliefs, our political systems, our national and racial divisions, limit our very numbers, junk or revise technologies so as to suit the law, then, brothers and sisters, we shall be immortal as no earlier man was or could be.

We shall evolve by our own more-knowing dreams; and where our line will abide in the universe, eons hence, no one can know but all will abet.

We have the necessary information for that end. It is information that also shows we must employ it or soon perish. For individuals, so far, have managed even an intellectual understanding of the necessity and its hope. Of those few, perhaps not one has clearly faced the implications of change their truth connotes—demands rather—and will exact of man if he acts rightly or exact as the cost of continuing evasion: the life of mankind, itself.

The times are frightening, of course.

And there are no fearless people. But people come in two kinds, the brave and the craven. Whoever is "fearless" has lost his humanity and is a lunatic. Fear tells the rest that what we cherish is in peril, but fear not say whether our evaluation is true or not. We can cherish false beliefs, our own selves, our one nation or synthetic God beyond species worth, for example. Thus, when we feel fear, it may lead to responses that, however brave, merely support some folly.

But that human being who feels fear and responds by acknowledging his condition, then seeking the cause of the peril and holding himself together during the next effort to remove a found danger, is, at least, *brave*. If his value-system is sound, he is, also, that best being any man or woman can realize.

The coward fails. To what is, or what he imagines a threat that relates to his values, he reacts inappropriately because he cannot admit fear and still manage both himself and that state. He becomes hysterical or panics. There is too much young hysteria and panic these days, and too much of it rises from fears that are not managed by courage; and those fears are too often based on a witless appraisal of self, others and reality.

The question before man, now, is this:

Has man that instinct for the survival of other species and if so, can he rearrange his bastard perversions of it, in all the current forms, *completely* and also quickly enough to survive, assuming he still has the chance?

Any other assumption is, of course, not valid.

No government has envisaged the problem. Our own, recently, has been blinder than prior administrations and even cut out many of the best eyes of scientific research for the end of, God save us, *economy!* The revolutionary kids have no idea how piddling and pointless their cause is measured, beside the revolution essential if any one is to live in a future, including the descendants of such "politicized" horses' asses.

So, I have come to that promised end of what, I'm sure will seem to many a heresy and to others a moral preachment but what is, in fact, only a lecture on ecology.

Man has been a heretic in nature and, now, as technological man, he stands at the a-biological pinnacle. He must put up or be shut up.

We do not send biologists to the White House yet; and our Presidents don't ask advice from them. Presidents and congressmen think that physicists and engineers are scientists and the main sort, because, alas, that's what nearly everybody else thinks.

So if there's a moral in this address, it's not mine but one implicit in truths thousands of others have patiently put together, truths concerning man and nature and man's nature. If that work suggests a "moral system" the system has governed life from the start and will to the end, irrespective of whether or not enough members of our breed can be converted to its truth. The knowledge is here. The implications are awesome, but they contain the first seed of hope man ever had to plant: something, where nothing was, before, that would sprout and could grow.

To know that, to sit in the quiet appreciation of the fact that one is lucky enough to be alive at that first moment when any man had even an optimistic possibility, is to experience the greatest exultation man ever could.

But it is also to see this is not the hour for demolition: we must learn, first, what to keep and what must be built that will be new; only then can we start destroying temples. It is not a time to go on believing some indescribable, inplausible and unprovable "God" is in charge of man or nature. It is not an opportunity for collective doctrines since man is not ruled by economics. But, since it *is* a time to be afraid, it is, in equal degree, a time for *courage*. And people are pretty brave.

If I have not conveyed to you my sense of this transcendent exhilaration, it is not owing to the lack of substance in what inspires me, and not . . . I believe . . . for my lack of trying.

You must take it from here, in any case.

And even that leaves me far from despair and, certainly, not in panic. The sighting of our possibility, that coast rising after man's million-year voyage on empty seas, is enough reward for the whole of journey, to us who are old.